THE LEGAL ASPECTS OF CENSORSHIP OF PUBLIC SCHOOL LIBRARY AND INSTRUCTIONAL MATERIALS

JOSEPH E. BRYSON
Professor of Education
The University of North Carolina
Greensboro, North Carolina

ELIZABETH W. DETTY
Director of Instruction and Personnel
Salisbury City Schools
Salisbury, North Carolina

THE MICHIE COMPANY
Law Publishers
CHARLOTTESVILLE, VIRGINIA

TABLE OF CONTENTS

Page

Preface v

CHAPTER 1. INTRODUCTION 1
§ 1.0. Overview 1
§ 1.1. Status of Censorship Practices in the Public
Schools 2
§ 1.2. Questions to be Answered 8
§ 1.3. Coverage and Organization of Issues Involved 9
§ 1.4. Definition of Terms 10

CHAPTER 2. REVIEW OF THE LITERATURE 13
§ 2.0. Introduction 13
§ 2.1. Historical Perspective on Censorship 14
§ 2.2. Censorship in the American Colonies 25
§ 2.3. Eighteenth-Century Censorship in America .. 28
§ 2.4. Censorship in Nineteenth and Twentieth
Century America 31
§ 2.5. Summary 69

CHAPTER 3. THE LEGAL ASPECTS OF CENSORSHIP OF PUBLIC
SCHOOL LIBRARY AND INSTRUCTIONAL MATERIALS 71
§ 3.0. Introduction 71
§ 3.1. A Framework for Analyzing Legal Aspects of
Censorship of Public School Library and
Instructional Materials 73
A. Academic Freedom of Public School Teachers 73
B. Right of Students to Read and Receive
Information 77
C. School Board Authority to Select and Remove
Library and Instructional Materials 81
D. Parents' Right to Direct Education of Children 85
E. Religious Freedom of Public School Students,
Related to Use of Library and Instructional
Materials 87
§ 3.2. Evolution of Legal Definition of Obscenity 92

                                                            Page
§ 3.3.   Censorship Cases 101
    A.   Cases Supporting School Board Action 101
    B.   Cases Supporting Constitutional Rights 116
§ 3.4.   Summary 134

CHAPTER 4.   REVIEW OF COURT DECISIONS 137
§ 4.0.   Introduction 137
§ 4.1.   Academic Freedom of Public School Teachers   139
§ 4.2.   Students' Rights to Read, Inquire, and Receive
         Information 151
§ 4.3.   Right of School Boards to Select and Remove
         Library and Instructional Materials 177
§ 4.4.   Parents' Right to Direct the Education of
         Children 187

CHAPTER 5.   SUMMARY, CONCLUSIONS, AND   RECOMMEN-
         DATIONS 197
§ 5.0.   Summary 198
§ 5.1.   Conclusions 202
§ 5.2.   Recommendations 204
§ 5.3.   Concluding Statement 209
§ 5.4.   Recommended School Board Policy for Selection
         of Library and Instructional Materials 210

Bibliography 217
Table of Cases 229
Index 237

PREFACE

An historical review indicates that censorship based on politics, religion and morality has been a continual issue throughout man's recorded history. The struggle for authority and control of people's minds and souls is always omnipresent. Arrogance, ignorance, dogma and absolute knowledge are some of the descriptive words in this struggle. The American settlers brought with them to the new world a heritage of suppression of reading matter by church and state. Censorship of obscenity in reading materials began in the early eighteenth century in the New England colonies. However, censorship did not emerge as a legal issue for over one hundred years—the early 1800s. From that time until the present, obscenity has been a serious judicial issue. Many organizations and groups have arisen to serve as prevaricating censors of library books, textbooks, and other educational materials. Opposing organizations have worked equally hard to prevent censorship and to protect the First and Fourteenth Amendments rights of students to read, to learn and to explore ideas. Fostering the Jeffersonian premise that a democracy cannot be both ignorant and free, anti-censorship advocates have promoted academic freedom of public school teachers and students. In 1814 Thomas Jefferson sought a French scientific publication from a Philadelphia book agent, and when informed that the book was unavailable because of religious censorship from authorities in Philadelphia, he wrote the following letter to his book agent N. G. Dufief:

> Is this then our freedom of religion? And are we to have a censor whose imprimatur shall say what books may be sold, and what we may buy? . . . Whose foot is to be the measure to which ours are all to be cut or stretched? Is a priest to be our inquisitor, or shall a layman, simple as ourselves, set up his reason as the rule for what we are to read, and what we must believe?

> It is an insult to our citizens to question whether they
> are rational beings or not, and blasphemy against
> religion to suppose it cannot stand the test of truth and
> reason. (Letter to N. G. Dufief dated April 19, 1814.)

This study presents an historical perspective of censorship in the United States. A definition of obscenity is
established as such definition evolved through the judiciary
from the nineteenth century until the present. The study
examines contemporary censorship problems relating to
public school library and instructional materials. Current
social, political, moral and religious issues central to censorship are delineated as those issues affect the public
schools. Recent surveys indicating the extent to which
schools are faced with censorship are examined.

A legal background is presented for the analysis of judicial decisions concerning censorship in five areas: (1) academic freedom of teachers; (2) students' right to read,
inquire, and receive information; (3) right of local school
boards to select and remove library and instructional materials; (4) parents' right to direct education of children; and
(5) religious freedom of public school students as it relates
to use of library and instructional materials.

Litigation concerning censorship in general influences
decisions on public school censorship. Landmark cases and
key studies relating to such litigation are reviewed in this
study in order to interpret major judicial issues.

Finally, the overall purpose of this study is to provide
appropriate information to aid educational decision makers
in matters concerning legal aspects of censorship.
Moreover, the information will assist in selection of appropriate educational materials and preparation of policies and
procedures. Proper selection, policies, and procedures

should help prevent litigation and adverse public relations
if and when censorship becomes an issue in school systems.

Greensboro, North Carolina   Joseph E. Bryson
June, 1982   Elizabeth W. Detty

Chapter 1

INTRODUCTION

§ 1.0. Overview.
§ 1.1. Status of Censorship Practices in the Public Schools.
§ 1.2. Questions to Be Answered.
§ 1.3. Coverage and Organization of Issues Involved.
§ 1.4. Definition of Terms.

§ 1.0. Overview.

A review of recent court cases establishes that censorship of educational materials in public schools is a real and present dilemma for educational leaders today. The current conservative political and moral climate and public dissatisfaction with taxes, foreign policy, busing, forced desegregation, and government in general have caused many people to flout public schools. Propinquity and familiarity make schools targets more accessible than federal, state, or even local government.[1] Well-organized groups, dissatisfied with public schools for many reasons and with excessive governmental control, are influencing citizens to crusade to "clean up" material presented to students. These groups focus criticism on books and other materials which present ideas they oppose in the areas of religion, politics, and morality.[2] In spite of criticism, public schools in a democratic society must provide students an opportunity to learn divergent points of view in controversial areas. Educators must attempt to support academic freedom.[3] At the same

---

1. Edward B. Jenkinson, "Dirty Dictionaries, Obscene Nursery Rhymes, and Burned Books," in *Dealing with Censorship, Teachers of English*, 1979, p. 5.

2. *Ibid.*

3. Thomas C. Hatcher, "Educational Directions in a Pluralistic Society," in *Indoctrinate or Educate?* eds. Thomas C. Hatcher and Lawrence

1

time educational leaders must promote good will and gain public support for financing schools and to retain students in public schools. Community involvement in schools can be a two-edged sword, providing support and interest on one side and criticism and interference on the other. School boards and administrators must be prepared through legal principles, appropriate philosophies, and clearly-defined guidelines to conduct educational programs of schools without being unduly swayed by pressure groups.[4]

A review of judicial decisions can help educational leaders understand the complexity of the issues and the schools' responsibility to provide appropriate instructional materials. It is also important that school decision makers understand who the censors are, who is behind censorship, and why censorship is prevalent at this time. Administrators need to be able to identify critical areas where censorship and court action may arise. Moreover, school administrations must be prepared to deal effectively with controversial issues before the school system and the educational process suffer considerable harm.

§ 1.1. Status of Censorship Practices in the Public Schools.

School districts currently faced with falling enrollment and public pressure for "back to basics" are confronted with the possiblility of an additional crisis—censorship of library and instructional materials.[5] When such crisis does occur,

G. Erickson (Newark, Del.: International Reading Association, 1979), p. 41; Todd Clark, "Editorial Reflections—Freedom to Teach and Learn: Our Responsibility," *Social Education* 39 (April 1975): 202-03.

4. American Library Association, "What to Do Before the Censor Comes—And After," *Newsletter on Intellectual Freedom* 21 (March 1972): 49-56.

5. "Removing Books from School: More Now Than Anytime in the Last 25 Years," *American School Board Journal* 166 (June 1979): 22; "Cen-

solving it on the local level may result in better community understanding of curriculum and school board policies concerning the materials selection process.[6] Unfortunately, the result more often is poor public relations and public irritation in school districts. If the controversy cannot be solved locally, it may result in lengthy judicial involvement. This study is designed to offer information that can contribute toward positive local solutions of censorship problems, thus avoiding litigation.

Censorship of school library and instructional materials has increased in the past decade. The Office for Intellectual Freedom of the American Library Association reports that during 1977 and 1978 more accounts of book censoring were received than in the previous twenty-five years.[7] Approximately three hundred incidents were reported in that two-year span. Ninety percent of these accounts concerned public schools. More than thirty percent of those who responded to the American Library Association's survey experienced pressure for censorship in 1977, a ten percent increase over a survey conducted in 1965. Parents were the source of the pressure for removing books in seventy-eight percent of the school cases.[8]

It is imperative that school administrators, school boards, and school personnel know and understand why schools are a current target for such attacks. The same conservatism that produced the "back to basics" movement is being directed toward schools in the form of censorship.[9] Edward

---

sorship on Rise Again in Schools," *U. S. News and World Report* 86 (June 1979): 51.

6. "Textbooks Censors: You Can Survive Their Ire and Extinguish Their Fire." *The Executive Educator* 1 (July 1979): 26.

7. *Ibid.*

8. *Ibid.*

9. James C. Hefley, *Textbooks on Trial,* (Wheaton, Ill.: Victor Books, 1976), p. 188.

B. Jenkinson, Indiana University, Chairman of the National Council of Teachers of English, explains the move toward censorship in the following manner:

> [s]chools are a convenient target for unhappy citizens. Many people feel that they cannot fight Washington, the state capitol, or even city hall. When they become unhappy because of inflation, federal or state laws, the so-called moral decline, or anything else, they want to lash out. But they don't always know how to attack the problems that really trouble them. So they vent their spleen upon the schools.[10]

School boards are accessible and hold public meetings. Schools are open to parents who can demand to see principals, teachers, or school librarians. According to Jenkinson, since newspapers, television, and the rest of the media have given schools so much attention, "taxpayers have a tendency to feel that almost everything that's wrong with society stems from the schools." [11] The *NEA Reporter* stated in 1980, "This year censorship efforts have been focused on text and library materials that are allegedly 'pornographic,' 'depressing,' 'anti-God,' 'anti-American,' and 'anti- family.' " [12]

To further complicate matters, not all censors are conservatives. Liberal groups have well-organized campaigns to pressure schools and publishers against the use of publication of "sexist" or "racist" books and materials.[13] Both groups, no matter what their intentions, may cause the removal of valuable teaching and learning tools from the hands of teachers and children.

School boards and school administrators need to have a

---

10. Jenkinson, "Dirty Dictionaries": p. 5.

11. *Ibid.*

12. *NEA Reporter* 19 (January/February 1980): 1.

13. Pamela Ellen Procuniar, "The Intellectual Rights of Children," *Wilson Library Bulletin* 51 (October 1976): 165-66.

clear understanding of the problem in order to set legally effective selection and complaint policies and procedures. Once policies and procedures have been adopted they should be followed explicitly in order to withstand pressures and to protect the rights of students to read, to learn, and to be informed. These same policies can help protect academic freedom of teachers of the school district.[14] Teachers and school librarians require protection in the selection of materials and in handling complaints. Without such support the fear of losing a position or legal involvement may cause them to become censors, fearing to select or use materials which may cause controversy.

With proper guidance, community concern can become a healthy influence rather than a deleterious one. Parents are involved in schools. Forming partnerships with parents and community leaders in reviewing curricula and materials has proved successful in many communities.[15]

It is well recognized that academic freedom is essential at the university level to enable students to search for truth, although censorship problems do occasionally arise even at the college level. Applying the same principle at the public school, pre-college level is often more difficult. Freedom of expression in public education is limited by community standards where financial and community support is committed.[16]

Public schools usually reflect community standards even though parents and educators do not always look at the educational   process   from   the   same   viewpoint.

14. Lee Burress, "A Brief Report of the 1977 NCTE Censorship Survey," in *Dealing with Censorship,* ed. James E. Davis (Urbana, Ill.: National Council of Teachers of English, 1979), p. 19.

15. "Censorship on Rise Again in Schools," *U. S. News and World Report* 86 (June 4, 1979): 51.

16. Todd Clark, "Editorial Reflections—Freedom to Teach and to Learn: Our Responsibility," *Social Education* 39 (April 1975): 202.

Dissatisfaction with falling Scholastic Aptitude Test scores, student discipline, moral decline, lack of patriotism, lack of respect for adults, and belief that American children cannot read and compute as well as their parents did in school, has caused a general lack of confidence in current educational programs. This loss of faith has resulted in attacks on various phases of some curricula as well as on specific books and instructional materials.[17] Although these attacks have sometimes been led by ultraconservative or extremely liberal groups, they might not have become troublesome controversies if the public had had more confidence in public education.

Current teaching philosophy provides students opportunity to inquire, to look at various sides of an issue, and to make decisions. This may be a questionable process for parents whose own education involved more traditional indoctrination. Herein lies a dichotomy—indoctrination of American middle-class values as opposed to teaching students to think and reason.[18]

The United States Supreme Court has made it clear that teachers and students do not shed their constitutional rights at the schoolhouse door. In *Tinker*[19] the Court maintained that "[i]t can hardly be argued that either students or teachers shed their constitutional rights ... at the schoolhouse gate."[20] The *Tinker* decision is interpreted by authorities such as Judith Krug of the Office for Intellectual Freedom of the American Library Association to mean: "The U. S. Supreme Court has laid to rest the concept of *in*

---

17. *Ibid.*

18. Procuniar, "The Intellectual Rights of Children," pp. 165-66.

19. Tinker v. Des Moines Indep. Community School Dist., 393 U.S. 503, 89 S. Ct. 733, 21 L. Ed. 2d 731 (1969).

20. *Ibid.*, p. 506.

loco parentis as it relates to the mind."[21] Other legal authorities still question the fact that children have the same constitutional rights as adults. For example, Justice Potter Stewart, concurring in *Tinker,* expressed doubt on this point: "I cannot share the Court's uncritical assumption that, school discipline aside, the First Amendment rights of children are co-extensive with those of adults."[22]

The Supreme Court, nevertheless, asserted in *Tinker:*

> In our system, State-operated schools may not be enclaves to totalitarianism. School offiicals do not possess absolute authority over their students. Students in school as well as out of school are "persons" under the Constitution. They are possessed of fundamental rights which the State must respect, just as they themselves must respect their obligations to the State.[23]

The 1973 *Miller*[24] decision led to an increase in censorship litigation on the local level. The United States Supreme Court declined to establish a national standard on what constitutes obscenity. State laws based on "community standards" were given guidelines by the Supreme Court in judging materials under consideration as obscene. The opinion stated: "We emphasize that it is not our function to propose regulatory schemes for the States. That must await their concrete legislative efforts."[25]

School boards and administrators should study judicial decisions concerning censorship matters as the rulings relate to the states' responsibility for education as opposed to a national constitutional standard. First Amendment

---

21. Monroe C. Cohen, ed. *Personal Liberty and Education* (New York: Citation Press, 1976), p. 85.

22. Tinker v. Des Moines Indep. Community School Dist., p. 515.

23. *Ibid.*, p. 511.

24. Miller v. California, 413 U.S. 15, 93 S. Ct. 2607, 37 L. Ed. 2d 419 (1973).

25. *Ibid.*

rights for academic freedom of teachers, students' rights to read and inquire, and parents' right to direct the education of children need to be understood. Furthermore, any distinctions made between adults and children as applied to constitutional rights to read, to know, and to be informed need the attention of school boards and administrators.

This study, then, is significant in that it provides educational leaders a comprehensive analysis of the legal aspects of censorship in the public schools. It offers educational decision makers historical perspective and legal guidelines in developing policy. The study provides direction to school districts when crisis censorship situations arise which could involve school districts in litigation.

§ 1.2. Questions to be Answered.

The major purpose of this historical study is to examine and analyze judicial decisions which could influence policy making as it relates to censorship in public schools.

It also examines forces and issues behind censorship problems in schools as well as legal guidelines for making decisions concerning selection and use of educational materials in public schools. Below are listed several key questions which need to be answered so that guidelines can be developed:

1. Under what circumstances are constitutional rights of students, teachers, or parents involved when a school district is faced with a censorship problem?

2. What are the major educational issues involved in censorship of school library and instructional materials?

3. Who are the pressure groups chiefly responsible for censorship?

4. Are there specific trends to be determined from analysis of court cases?

5. Based on precedents established by "landmark" cases, what are legally acceptable criteria which are most likely to

assist school districts in preventing legal action and/or poor public relations in censorship cases?

§ 1.3. Coverage and Organization of Issues Involved.

The remainder of the study is divided into three major parts. Chapter 2 reviews literature related to the history of censorship and the effect of history on censorship of school library and instructional materials in the present. Furthermore, Chapter 2 traces the growth of community concern for school curricula and instructional materials which has led to censorship controversies. Also included is a summary of recent surveys which indicate the extent to which public schools are faced with censorship problems.

Chapter 3 contains an historical narrative of major legal issues relating to censorship of school library and instructional materials in five categories: (1) academic freedom of public school teachers, (2) students' right to read, inquire, and receive information, (3) school board authority to select and remove library and instructional materials, (4) parents' right to direct education of children, and (5) religious freedom of public school students as it relates to library and instructional materials. Chapter 3 also traces the development of the legal definition of obscenity. Further, Chapter 3 presents school censorship cases since 1965 in two categories: (1) cases upholding school board authority to select or remove library and instructional materials and (2) cases supporting constitutional rights of students and teachers in the use of library and instructional materials.

Chapter 4 is a discussion and analysis of major cases relating to the five categories identified in Chapter 3. Facts of the cases, decisions of the courts, and discussions of the cases are presented for each category.

The concluding Chapter 5 of the study contains a summary of the information obtained from review of the literature and from analysis of selected court cases. The questions asked in the introductory part of the study are reviewed and answered in this concluding chapter. Recommendations for formulation of legally acceptable policies concerning selection of library and instructional materials are made. Finally, procedures for handling complaints concerning challenged materials are included.

§ 1.4. Definition of Terms.

For the purpose of this study, the following selected terms are defined:

Censorship. — A process which limits access to books and materials based on value judgments or prejudices of individuals or groups. The act of censorship may be accomplished by (1) suppression of use, (2) removal of books or materials from the library or classroom, or (3) limiting access of library and instructional materials. Censorship withholds or limits the students' right to read, to learn, and to be informed and the teachers' right to academic freedom.

Censor. — One who prevents the adoption or continued use of specific library and instructional materials in public schools. The censor may be a parent, student, school board member, school administrator, teacher, librarian, clergyman, local citizen, member of the community, or representative of a local or national organization. The censor bases his act on value judgment or personal prejudice founded on social, political, moral, or religious views.

Selection. — A process whereby specific books and materials are chosen from all available materials. Decisions are based on appropriateness for the users, educational considerations, balance of presentation, budgetary matters, and available space.

Academic Freedom. — A concept whereby teaching and learning necessitate freedom to teach, study, and discuss divergent ideas, philosophies, and opinions; making decisions and developing beliefs from study; and expression of

10

ideas thus formed, publicly as well as privately. For public school teachers and students, academic freedom involves use of books and other materials in classrooms and libraries which present various points of view. The philosophy of a balance in presentation is inherent in the concept.

Obscenity. — The following is the definition of obscenity asserted by the Supreme Court in 1973. It has been used by the courts in the United States since that time:

> (a) whether the average person, applying contemporary community standards would find that a work, taken as a whole, appeals to the prurient interest, (b) whether a work depicts or describes, in a patently offensive way, sexual conduct specifically defined by applicable state law, and (c) whether the work taken as a whole, lacks serious literary, artistic, political, or scientific value.[26]

---

26. Miller v. California, 413 U.S. p. 24.

Chapter 2

REVIEW OF THE LITERATURE

§ 2.0. Introduction.
§ 2.1. Historical Perspective on Censorship.
§ 2.2. Censorship in the American Colonies.
§ 2.3. Eighteenth-Century Censorship in America.
§ 2.4. Censorship in Nineteenth and Twentieth Century America.
§ 2.5. Summary.

§ 2.0. Introduction.

Censorship has been with mankind since early recorded history. Although a complete review of literature pertaining to censorship is unnecessary and impractical, an historical perspective is presented to give the reader a world overview of this pervasive subject. This background shows how censorship practices came to be accepted in colonial America and thus in the United States.

Early censorship involved suppression of written material chiefly in the areas of religious and political thought. It was not until the nineteenth century that obscenity and morality became real issues in the courts.

As literacy increased among the common people, more books were published and eventually became available in less expensive editions; legal actions concerning censorship expanded correspondingly. The susceptibility of youth and common man to the evils of obscenity and controversy in the areas of politics and religion have thus been litigious issues of increasing importance and frequency.

Censorship in the United States in the twentieth century has involved many areas of society. However, for the purpose of this study, major attention has been given to that involving public schools.

In recent years censorship of public school library and instructional materials has been on the rise in the United

13

States. The results of recent surveys substantiate this fact. This chapter also focuses on involvement of organized groups and members of the community as they attempt to restrain freedom of thought. This restraint has taken the form of suppression of or limiting access to public school library and instructional materials.

§ 2.1. Historical Perspective on Censorship.

Early History.

Since the beginning of human history man has used fire as a symbol of disapproval and cleansing.[1] The destruction of written works considered offensive to authority has been recorded as early as Old Testament times. The Book of Jeremiah describes the burning of a scroll by King Jehoiakim in Jerusalem.[2] Condemning the scroll to fire was the king's expression of displeasure with Jeremiah's prophecy which predicted a sad future for the kingdom.[3] Burning is always the most severe form of censorship.

Throughout human history, basic disagreements in attitudes toward philosophy, morality, politics, and religion have brought with them the plague of censorship. Plato's *Dialogues* rejected the use of bad fiction with children:

> And shall we just carelessly allow children to hear any casual tales which may be devised by casual persons, and receive into their minds ideas for the most part the very opposite of those which we should wish them to have when they are grown up?
>
> We cannot.
>
> Then the first thing will be to establish a censorship

---

1. Charles Ripley Gillett, *Burned Books: Neglected Chapters in British History and Literature,* 2 vols. (New York: Columbia University Press, 1932), 1:3.
2. Jeremiah 35:9-12 (RSV).
3. *Ibid.*

of the writers of fiction, and let the censors receive any tale of fiction which is good, and reject the bad. . . .[4]

Poetry also provoked Plato's criticism. The idolization of Homer and the reading of poetry endangered "law and reason" and, as a result, endangered the state.[5]

The state was of utmost importance in ancient Greece and Rome. An attack on the gods, who were central to these cultures and their politics, was interpreted as an attack on the state rather than on religion.[6] Consequently, censorship became a means of suppressing political thought.[7]

The ancient civilization of China also had its book

---

4. Plato, *The Republic, The Dialogues of Plato,* 2 vols. trans. B. Jowett (New York: Oxford University Press, 1892) 2:323.

5. *Ibid.* See also Carl Sagan, *COSMOS* (New York, Random House, 1980) especially Chapter VII. Professor Sagan develops an intriguing historical analysis of conflict between practical scientific philosophers and moral philosophers. Such was the case when the Ionian school of scientific philosophers (so called in the history of philosophy as the Pre-Socratics) Thales, Anaximander, Pythagoras, Theodocus, Hippocrates, Democritus, Anaxagoras and others collided with the Athenian metaphysical school led by Socrates, Plato, and Aristotle — especially Plato and Aristotle. Democritus becomes a major example in the conflict. In the Graeco-Roman world Democritus enjoyed a philosophical reputation almost equal to Plato and Aristotle. He was a learned scholar, philosophical genius and possessed an able literary style comparable to Plato's dialogues. Democritus wrote more than seventy books; yet, only fragments exist today. Professor Wilhelm Windelband in the History of Ancient Philosophy (English translated at p. 172) suggests "the most lamentable (loss) that has happened to the original documents of ancient history." History suggests that Plato urged the burning of Democritus' books; perhaps, because Democritus' cosmology did not agree with Plato's "Doctrine of the Ideal of the Supreme Form." See also Benjamin Farrington, *Greek Science,* London: Penquin 1953; and B. A. G. Fuller, *A History of Philosphy* (New York: Henry Holt and Company, 1945).

6. Morris L. Ernst and William Seagle, *To the Pure . . . A Study of Obscenity and the Censor* (New York: Viking, 1928), p. 16.

7. *Ibid.,* p. 27.

burners. Hwangti, the monarch who built the Great Wall, believed ". . . when men become too wise they become worthless." [8] Because of this belief, he caused the destruction of all the literature of China except that dealing with medicine, science, and agriculture. Further, he executed or expelled many authors and scholars.[9]

Early Christians, in embracing their new philosophy, were prompted to burn any of their own books opposed to the teachings of Jesus. "And a number of those who practiced magic arts brought their books together and burned them in the sight of all." [10]

Only a few books in the famous library in Alexandria, Egypt, escaped destruction when Omar, leader of the Moslems, captured the city in A. D. 642. It is reported that as many as 700,000 volumes (many of which were painstakingly collected form other centers of learning) were burned. The unnecessary destruction of these manuscripts was an early form of mass censorship. Historical records indicate the scrolls were used to heat the four thousand baths of the city for at least six months.[11] Some historians report that Omar believed that knowledge contained in the Koran was sufficient for man. If a book agreed with the Koran, it was unnecessary. If it opposed the Koran, it was unnecessary. If it opposed the Koran, it should be destroyed.[12]

Censorship and the Church in Rome.

At the Council of Nice in A. D. 325, the first formal

---

8. George W. Lyon, "Book Burners in History," *The Saturday Review* 25 (August 15, 1942): 12.

9. *Ibid.*

10. Acts 19:19 (RSV).

11. Lyon, "Book Burners in History," p. 12. See also Carl Sagan, *COSMOS* (New York: Random House, 1980, p. 12-20, 332-37).

12. *Ibid.*

approach to book censorship was taken by the Roman Catholic Church. The teachings of Arius and his book, *Thalia*, were the initial target for the Council's condemnation.[13] In A. D. 405, Pope Innocent I sent the Bishop of Toulouse a list of "authentic books of the Bible and listed a number of apocryphal documents that were condemned." [14]

In the era before the printing press was invented, written works were in manuscript form. Since few copies were available, the complete destruction of a written work was relatively simple. After the invention of movable type in the middle of the fifteenth century, such destruction became more difficult.[15]

In 1524, Charles V of Belgium is reputed to have published the first list of forbidden books by the Roman Catholic Church.[16] This list was drawn up under clerical advice. Heresy, not morality, was the basis for condemning books by the Church in Rome.[17]

The famous *Index Librorum Prohibitorum* was compiled in 1559 by Pope Paul IV. The *Index* was divided into three lists: (1) authors whose entire works were forbidden; (2) specific works prohibited; and (3) forbidden works by anonymous authors. The *Index* was published in 1564 at the close of the Council of Trent after theological faculties from all over Europe had been consulted.[18]

---

13. Redmond A. Burke, *What Is the Index?* (Milwaukee: Brace Publishing Co., 1952), p. 5.

14. *Ibid.*

15. Robert B. Downs, ed., *The First Freedom: Liberty and Justice in the World of Books and Reading* (Chicago: American Library Association, 1960), p. 2.

16. Edmund Gosse, "The Censorship of Books," *English Review* 4 (March 1910): 622.

17. *Ibid.*, p. 623.

18. *Ibid.*, p. 622.

While some Popes condemned books, others encouraged the writing of many works, including obscenity. Pope Nicholas V, for example, brought to Rome, Francisco Filelfo, "a perfect master in the art of scurrilous vituperation." [19] In a similar vein, Valla, who wrote allegedly obscene satire on religion, was asked to translate Thucydides' works into Latin. [20] It should be pointed out that during this same Renaissance period, many Roman priests were engaged in copying and preserving various types of worthy literature.

Licensing of books was required by Pope Innocent VIII "to prevent publication of any works presenting an erroneous interpretation of Catholic doctrine." [21] The Council of Trent (1545-1563) appointed a Council to judge all publications. The Council lasted for almost four hundred years. [22]

The most celebrated scientific literature censorship case of the Renaissance and Reformation encapsulated Copernicus, Galileo and Pope Urban VIII Maffeo Barberini. This story begins in 1543 when Copernicus (1473-1543), a distinguished Christian churchman and intellectual humanist, by now approaching seventy years of life, published *The Revolutions of Heavenly Spheres.* [23] The book

---

19. Ludwig Pastor, *The History of the Popes from the Close of the Middle Ages* (St. Louis: B. Hurder, 1898), p. 197.

20. *Ibid.*

21. *Ibid.*

22. Burke, *What Is the Index?*, p. 7.

23. Nicolaus Copernicus, *The Revolution of Heavenly Spheres*, University of Chicago, Great Books of the Western World, Encyclopedia Britannica, Inc. Robert M. Hutchins, Editor in Chief, 1952, Volume 16, pp. 499-837; Copernicus dedicated the book to Pope Paul III. The opening sentence establishes a questionable concern:

> Since the newness of the hypotheses of this work—which sets the earth in motion and puts an immovable sun at the center of the universe — has already received a great deal of publicity, I have no doubt that certain of the savants have taken grave offense and think

is Copernicus' mathematical descriptions of the universe with the sun at center and planets circling the sun.

Copernicus developed the theory early in life — perhaps age forty—but due to the religious revolution and Counter-Reformation withheld publication. The Roman Catholic Church had long accepted the Ptolemy concept, supported by Artistotle's cosmology and philosophy, that earth was universally centered and the sun moved around the earth.[24] Even though Copernicus died the year his book was published it is reported that he saw a copy.[25] In 1616 the Roman Catholic Church banned Copernicus' book " 'until corrected.' " Censorship, although never effective, was lifted in 1835.

Both horns of the universal dilemma are now identified—the Roman Catholic Church holds to an earth-centered universe and Copernicus has postulated a sun-centered universe. Galileo enters the dilemma at this point. Galileo early had established himself Europe's leading scientist. After examining the starry heavens through his own telescope he realized that Ptolemaic cosmology would not work. Copernicus had been right and Galileo intended to right a great injustice. His strategy was to play for time—the right moment—to reveal to everyone Copernicus' simple truth and to present the concept so persuasively and the proof would be so overwhelming that no one could disbelieve.[26] How wrong Galileo was.

Galileo, during the next twenty years, visited Rome on two occasions, seeking to persuade church authorities to

---

it wrong to raise any disturbance among liberal disciplines which have had the right set-up for a long time now.

24. Jacob Bronowski, *The Ascent of Man* (Boston: Little, Brown and Company, 1973), pp. 196, 199. See also Carl Sagan, *COSMOS* (New York: Random House, 1980), pp. 57-62.

25. *Ibid.*, p. 197.

26. *Ibid.*, p. 204.

allow Copernicus' theory to flow into the mainstream of ecclesiastical thinking. The first trip was in 1616 where he intended using his influence among the Cardinals not to suppress Copernican cosmology. But Galileo is much too late. The struggle for absolute authority and control is always more important to institutions than new ideas. The Roman Catholic Church Counter-Reformation was underway. The judgmental logic is so simple—those not for us are against us—a heretic. Galileo is prohibited from holding and/or defending the Copernican view — "That the sun is immovable at the center of the heaven." [27]

In 1624 Galileo again traveled to Rome and on six occasions visited with the new Pope Urban VIII Maffeo Barberini in the Vatican gardens. For some unknown reason Galileo mistakenly believed that Pope Urban VIII (who had a reputation as a Cardinal as being an intellectual and who loved art, science, and music) would support him. So in 1632 Galileo published the *Dialogue on the Two Principal Systems of the World.* Pope Urban VIII was outraged and he insisted that Galileo had "ventured to meddle with things that he ought not to." [28] The book was banned and all copies must be collected. In 1633 Galileo was summoned to Rome. The trial began and Galileo early on agreed to recant.

> [A]nd after it had been notified to me that the said doctrine was contrary to Holy Scripture—I wrote and printed a book in which I discuss this doctrine already condemned and adduce arguments of great cogency in its favor. . . .
>
> Therefore, designing to remove from the minds of your Eminences, and of all faithful Christians, . . . I abjure, curse, and detest the aforesaid errors and

---

27. *Ibid.*, p. 207.
28. *Ibid.*, p. 209.

heresies, . . . I, Galileo Galilei, have abjured as above with my own hand.[29]

Galileo was condemned to house arrest for life. On leaving Rome, in 1633, he was allowed to return to his villa at Arcetri, near Florence where he spent the remainder of his life working on scientific investigations. In 1638 he published the *Dialogue of the Two New Sciences,* which Galileo insisted was "superior to everything else of mine hitherto published." [30] The book was published by Protestants in the Netherlands. Even though Galileo became blind in late 1637 he continued scientific investigations and correspondence until his death January 8, 1642.

One of the most interesting book burners of the Renaissance was Dominican Savonarola, a monk and reformer who lived in Florence. Not only was he an eloquent preacher with persuasive powers (he is reputed to have converted a large segment of Florence's population between 1494-1498) but had political ambition as well. He criticized the established political authority and developed an elaborate spy system to keep an eye on the private life of Florence. Such was Savonarola's power that he was able to confiscate, with force, books and art work which he did not approve. Savonarola reached the pinnacle of power in 1497 with one of history's most dramatic book burning events. He gathered books and manuscripts (some from outstanding authors' pens such as Boccaccio, Pulic, and Petrarch), paintings and statues, music instruments, playing cards and other games and body adornment articles for a public burning. What makes this story so significant is that one

---

29. *Ibid.,* p. 217.

30. Galileo Galilei, *Dialogue of the Two New Sciences,* University of Chicago, Great Books of the Western World, Encyclopedia Britannica, Inc. (Robert M. Hutchins, Editor in Chief, 1952) Volume 28, pp. 127-250.

year later, the church excommunicated him, the new political authority condemned him and the fickle populas that had so praised him and cheered him on just a year before, assisted in burning Savonarola on the very same spot.[31]

This brief historical look at censorship during the Renaissance would not be complete unless there is recognition of those who paid the ultimate price—burned at the stake—for freedom of inquiry. Guiordano Bruno (1548-1600) is representative. Bruno, a contemporary of both Copernicus and Galileo, was a philosopher and scientist of the highest magnitude. Influenced by Neo-Platonic mysticism and the new Aristotalianism and postulating Copernican astronomy, Bruno published numerous books and lectured widely on the Continent, London and Oxford.[32]

Even though he began his career as a Dominican monk, he later rejected both Catholicism and the new Protestantism. And in his later publications especially the allegory entitled *Spaccio della Bestia Trionfante (Expulsion of the Triumphant Beast)* attacked Christianity, and compared the Old Testament with Greek mythology.[33] Not only was Bruno's book burned but in 1593 he accepted an invitation to return to Venice and was betrayed to the Inquisition. After a lengthy trial he was imprisoned and in 1600 burned at the stake—the ultimate price for an idea and freedom of thought.[34]

In 1948 the last official reading list of the Roman Catholic Church was published. It included many masterpieces of the Western world. After many centuries, Church control

---

31. B. A. G. Fuller, *A History of Philosophy* (New York: Henry Holt and Company, 1945), p. 10.

32. B. A. G. Fuller, *A History of Philosophy* (New York: Henry Holt and Company, 1945), p. 31. See also Frederick Mayer, *A History of Modern Philosophy* (New York: American Book Company, 1951), pp. 65-69.

33. *Ibid.*

34. *Ibid.*

over reading by Roman Catholics officially ceased in 1966 when publication of the *Index* ceased.[35]

English Censorship: Sixteenth and Seventeenth Centuries.

Censorship in England during the Reformation involved heresy against the state as well as against religion. The writings of Martin Luther were publicly burned in Cambridge in 1520 to show disapproval by Cardinal Thomas Wolsey. In 1521 London was the scene of a similar burning of Luther's works by John Fisher, Bishop of Rochester.[36] Henry VIII issued a list of eighteen forbidden books, five by Martin Luther. His list, however, did not prevent the reading of the author's works.[37]

During the sixteenth century, England was the scene of many book burnings and seizures. In 1556 the Stationers' Company was the exclusive printer for England. Search and seizure of printers, binders, and sellers of books was a common event carried on in the name of the state and religion.[38] In 1559 Queen Elizabeth decreed that a license must be bought in order to engage in the publication of printed materials.

The First Quarto of William Shakespeare's play, *Richard the Second,* was published by the Stationers' Company in 1597 and the next two quartos were printed in 1598. At that time Queen Elizabeth I was extremely sensitive about the uncertainty of her successor to the throne and about the various factions who favored a number of candidates. A

---

35. Anne Lyon Haight, *Banned Books: Informal Notes on Some Books Banned for Various Reasons at Various Times and in Various Places* (New York: Bowker, 1970), p. 109.

36. Gillett, *Burned Books,* 1:19.

37. *Ibid.,* 1:20.

38. Norman St. John-Stevas, *Obscenity and the Law* (London: Secker and Warburg, 1956), p. 6.

scene from the play depicting Richard II's deposition so angered the Queen that she ordered the scene expurgated. Fear of her further wrath prevented publication of Act IV, Scene I, lines 154-318, until 1608 after her death. The scene reads in part as Richard II speaks:

> Now mark me, how I will undo myself.
> I give this heavy weight from off my head
> and this unwieldy sceptre from my hand,
> The pride of kingly sway from out my heart.
> With mine own tears I wash away my balm,
> With mine own hands I give away my crown,
> With mine own tongue deny my sacred state,
> With mine own breath release all duteous oaths.
> All pomp and majesty I do forswear;
> My manors, rents, revenues I forgo;
> My acts, decrees, and statutes I deny.
> God pardon all oaths that are broke to me!
> God keep all vows unbroke are made to thee! [39]

The absence of the scene is an example of the fear created by the power of the throne over publications in England during the sixteenth century.

The Star Chamber period of England was one of almost complete suppression. In 1641 the English Parliament abolished the Star Chamber and the English common courts were expanded. For a short period there were no censorship laws; however, less than three years later Cromwell again called for licensing of publications to prevent religious abuse.[40] The following year the English poet, John Milton, fought for the right to print and publish without a license. His was a personal defense since he had published several

---

39. William Shakespeare, *The Complete Plays and Poems of William Shakespeare,* ed. William Allen Neilson and Charles Jarvis Hill, *The Tragedy of Richard the Second* (Cambridge, Mass.: Houghton Mifflin Co., 1942), p. 623.

40. St. John-Stevas, *Obscenity and the Law,* p. 8.

unlicensed pamphlets on divorce.[41] In *Areopagitica,* Milton wrote:

> Who kills a man kills a reasonable creature, God's image; but he who destroys a good book, kills reason itself, kills the image of God, as it were in the eye. A good book is the precious life blood of a master spirit, embalmed and treasured up on purpose to a life beyond.[42]

The Printing Act of 1662 in England limited all printing to the Stationers' Company of London and to Cambridge and Oxford Universities. This law prohibited the publication in England of any books offensive to the faith of the Church of England or seditious toward the government. Because the law was difficult to enforce, however, it was abandoned when it expired in 1695.[43]

§ 2.2. Censorship in the American Colonies.

The first settlers came to the new world from countries where licensing was required for printing and where church and state intervention was an everyday occurrence. Having fled from injustices which included the suppression of freedom of speech and religion, it might be presumed that colonists would establish such freedom in the new land. Such was not the case. Instead, early censorship in America reflected the historical suppression of the settlers' diverse backgrounds. The main features of the English licensing system became the standard for most of the colonies in America.[44] Such restrictions were warmly supported by the

---

41. John Milton, *Paradise Lost and Selected Poetry and Prose,* ed. Northrop Frye (New York: Rinehart and Co., 1951), p. 464.

42. *Ibid.*

43. Robert W. Haney, *Comstockery in America: Patterns of Censorship and Control* (Boston: Beacon Press, 1960), p. 14.

44. Paul Blanshard, *The Right to Read: The Battle Against Censorship* (Boston: Beacon Press, 1955), p. 32.

British colonial governors as protection against rebellion.[45]

Puritanism, as practiced in the New England colonies, was an outgrowth of Calvinism.[46] Literary historian Percy Boynton describes the Puritan as "narrowly orthodox" in his religion. He writes further:

> He was a cruel man, living in a cruel age in the fear of a cruel God. He had no qualms about subjecting other men to the rigors of the bilboes or the whipping post, to the tortures of branding and maiming, to treating women of unruly tongue to a swing on the ducking stool or a taste of the gag or the cleft stick, and to humiliating both men and women in the stocks or the pillory, with public rebuke in church or the stigma of the scarlet letter.[47]

The middle colonies were populated by settlers with greater diversity in religious faith than the New England Colonies. For this reason, perhaps, their repression of literature was not as severe as that of their northern neighbors.[48]

The Massachusetts Bay Colony, on the other hand, included literary censorship as part of its police power.[49] Many colonists in Massachusetts were well educated and respected the power of the printed word; however, these attributes were limited by religious bigotry and moral orthodoxy.[50]

Presses were tightly controlled by colonial governors. The

---

45. *Ibid.*, p. 33.

46. Eli M. Oboler, *The Fear of the Word: Censorship and Sex* (Metuchen, New Jersey: The Scarecrow Press, 1974), pp. 64-65.

47. Percy H. Boynton, *Literature and American Life* (Boston: Ginn, 1936), p. 22.

48. Blanshard, *The Right to Read*, p. 33.

49. *Ibid.*

50. Ralph Edward McCoy, *Banned in Boston: The Development of Literary Censorship in Massachusetts* (Ph.D. dissertation, University of Illinois, 1956), pp. 2-3.

first printing press was established by Stephen Daye in 1638 in the Massachusetts Bay Colony. At least one bookstore was opened in 1652 and eight were in existence as early as 1686.[51]

Nevertheless, there was suppression of what could be read, controversial religious literature being the chief target. In 1650 a theological pamphlet, *The Meritorious Prince of Our Redemption,* by William Pynchon of Springfield, was the target of the first serious confrontation involving censorship. The General Court, the legislative body of the colony, ordered the pamphlet burned in the Boston marketplace.[52]

Roger Williams fled the Massachusetts Bay Colony when he could no longer tolerate the authority of government "over conscience." He founded the town of Providence in Rhode Island as a haven for freedom of religion and speech.[53]

As early as 1654 the General Court of Massachusetts, objecting to the beliefs and teachings of the Society of Friends, ordered that Quaker books be burned.[54] In 1662 this same legislative body limited printing to the Harvard College Press in Cambridge.[55] The papal doctrine of the *Imitation of Christ,* by Thomas a Kempis, was refused American publication in 1669. It had to be revised to suit local religious belief before it could be accepted.[56]

The first known attack on obscenity in Massachusetts occurred in 1668 with the censorship of Henry Neville's *Isle*

---

51. *Ibid.,* p. 2.
52. Haney, *Comstockery in America,* p. 17.
53. Haight, *Banned Books,* p. 25.
54. Haney, *Comstockery in America,* p. 17.
55. McCoy, *Banned in Boston,* p. 4.
56. Haney, *Comstockery in America,* p. 17.

of Pines.[57] The book was a humorous and sexually promiscuous story of an Englishman, George Pine, who professed to have been shipwrecked on an island with four young women.[58] A printer, Marmaduke Johnson, put forth an unlicensed edition of the book and was fined as a result.[59] Since Johnson's offense was actually one of publishing without a license, and since he was known locally as a troublemaker, it was not clearly an obscenity case.[60]

§ 2.3. Eighteenth-Century Censorship in America.

Shortly after the *Isle of Pines* incident, in 1711, "An Act against Intemperance, Immorality, and Profaneness, and for Reformation of Manners," was passed to prohibit the publication of obscene materials in the Massachusetts Bay Colony.[61]

The 1711 Massachusetts obscenity act and an obscenity law legislated in Vermont at about the same time were adopted prior to similar legislation in England.[62] It was the English common law, however, that established the early precedence in the courts of the United States.[63] This matter will be discussed in greater detail in nineteenth-century censorship.

Official licensing continued well into the eighteenth century in Massachusetts, although little official action was

---

57. Felice Flanery Lewis, *Literature, Obscenity, and Law* (Carbondale and Edwardsville: Southern Illinois University Press), p. 2.

58. *Ibid.*, pp. 2-3.

59. *Ibid.*, p. 3.

60. *Ibid.*

61. *Ibid.*

62. *Ibid.*, pp. 4-5.

63. *Ibid.*

actually taken against recalcitrant printers.[64] Few restrictions were imposed on the importation and sale of books from abroad except when there was explicit conflict with Puritan doctrine.[65]

Although other colonies were more tolerant than the Massachusetts Bay Colony, they also fostered governmental supervision of the press as well as intolerance of minority religious groups.[66] In spite of the early Massachusetts and Vermont obscenity laws, courts in colonial days and in the first era of American independence did little to curb sexual ideas through censorship of obscenity. During the earliest years, the United States inherited from its colonial beginnings an active history of censorship for sedition and heresy, but little for obscenity.[67]

The main progress toward freedom of the press in the colonial period was made by newspapers. Two major incidents during this period were the cases of James Franklin of Massachusetts and John Peter Zenger of New York. James Franklin was jailed in Massachusetts for expressing personal political views in his paper, *The New England Courant*. Franklin was released from jail by the Massachusetts court in 1722.[68] Soon after this, the landmark *Zenger* case in 1734 in New York helped establish freedom of the press that engaged in criticizing governmental authorities.[69] Primarily as a result of these two

---

64. Lawrence C. Wroth, "Printing in the Colonial Period, 1638-1703," ed. Lehmann-Haupt, *The Book in America* (New York: Bowker, 1951), p. 46.

65. Worthington C. Ford, *Boston Book Market, 1697-1700* (Boston: The Club of Odd Volumes, 1917), pp. 57-58.

66. Wroth, "Printing in the Colonial Period, 1638-1703," p. 43.

67. Morris L. Ernst and Alan U. Schwartz, *Censorship: The Search for the Obscene* (New York: Macmillan Co., 1964), p. 7.

68. Lewis, *Literature, Obscenity, and Law*, p. 4.

69. *Ibid.*

cases, freedom of newspapers from censorship was generally accepted when American colonies became independent. However, the same freedom was not extended to other forms of printed matter.[70]

In 1787 when delegates from the new states met in Philadelphia at the Constitutional Convention, George Washington and Benjamin Franklin presided over four months of secret sessions. James Madison made copious notes on the meetings.[71] The notes indicate that no mention was made of freedoms relating to religion, press, or speech. Furthermore, the new Constitution did not mention these freedoms until the First Amendment was added.

According to Chaffee "the original Constitution contained a considerable number of safeguards for human rights and was consequently equivalent to a bill of rights even though it did not carry the name." [72] On the other hand, Thomas Jefferson did not believe the Constitution sufficiently protected human rights. On December 20, 1787, Mr. Jefferson wrote from Paris to James Madison concerning omissions from the newly formed Constitution:

> I will now tell you what I do not like. First, the omission of a bill of rights, providing clearly, and without the aid of sophism, for freedom of religion, freedom of the press, protection against standing armies, restriction of monopolies, the eternal and unremitting force of the habeas corpus laws, and trials by jury in all matters of fact triable by the laws of the land, and not by laws of nations. . . . Let me add, that a bill of rights is what the people are entitled to against every government on earth, general or particular, and what no government should refuse, or rest on inference.[73]

---

70. *Ibid.*

71. Ernst and Schwartz, *Censorship,* p. 7.

72. Zechariah Chaffee, Jr., *Documents of Fundamental Human Rights* (New York: Atheneum, 1963) 1:4.

73. Saul K. Padover, ed., *The Writings of Thomas Jefferson* (New York: Heritage, 1967), pp. 311-12.

In 1791, the first ten amendments to the Constitution, the Bill of Rights, were adopted. On the basis of the First Amendment, many legal decisions influencing human rights have been made; these are basically the rights which guarantee the free interchange of ideas.

In spite of the separation from England, British legal precedents continued to have a strong influence on the courts in the United States.[74] Statutory censorship laws did not develop in this country until the nineteenth century.

§ 2.4. Censorship in Nineteenth and Twentieth Century America.

Nineteenth Century

Colonial America was a pioneer in controlling obscene literature since both Massachusetts and Vermont had adopted obscenity laws before England enacted similar legislation. Yet, English common law was the basis for decisions in the two earliest cases in the United States.[75] The English courts framed three criteria for obscenity: (1) intent of the accused; (2) corruption of youth; and (3) disturbance of the peace.[76] The latter two criteria have figured prominently in American judicial history. All three were considerations in the first two obscenity cases cited below.

The first known ruling of a United States court to establish precedent concerning censorship was in 1815. The case, *Commonwealth of Pennsylvania v. Sharpless,*[77] involved exhibiting a painting described as a "lewd and obscene painting, representing a man in an obscene, impudent, and

---

74. Ernst and Schwartz, *Censorship,* pp. 8-9.
75. Lewis, *Literature, Obscenity, and Law,* p. 4.
76. *Ibid.,* p. 5.
77. 2 S. & R. 91 (Pa. Sup. Ct. 1815).

31

indecent posture with a woman." [78] This case merits mention for two reasons. First, Pennsylvania had no obscenity law until 1860. Second, the case was decided on the principle of English common law and books were mentioned by dictum only.[79] The case was referred to the Pennsylvania Supreme Court from a lower court, and Sharpless was found guilty.

The second case, *Holmes*,[80] in 1821, involved the book, *Memoirs of a Woman of Pleasure,* currently known as *Fanny Hill.* The case was heard in Massachusetts and the decision was determined on English common-law principle. As for the three criteria framed by English law, the court stated: (1) intent of accused: "a scandalous and evil deposed person" (speaking of the author); (2) corruption of youth: "contriving, devising and intending, the morals as well as youth as of other good citizens of said commonwealth to debauch and corrupt, and to raise and create in their minds inordinate and lustful desires"; and (3) disturbance of the peace: "against the peace." [81] In both of the above cases judges directed their attention to disputed points of law upon which the appeals were based, instead of addressing the issue of whether the painting and novel were in fact obscene.[82] The judges seemed to "tacitly assume ... that obscenity was readily recognizable beyond doubt or question." [83] Moreover, there apparently was no question in their

---

78. Edward De Grazia, *Censorship Landmarks* (New York: Bowker, 1969), p. 39.

79. Curtis Bok, "Commonwealth v. Gordon et al.," in *The First Freedom: Liberty and Justice in the World of Books and Reading,* ed. Robert B. Downs (Chicago: American Library Association, 1960), pp. 100-01.

80. Commonwealth v. Holmes, 17 Mass. (1821).

81. *Ibid.,* p. 336.

82. Lewis, *Literature, Obscenity, and Law,* p. 6.

83. *Ibid.*

minds whether or not they had authority to ban obscene materials.[84]

Judge Curtis Bok discussed these two decisions in the case of *Gordon*[85] in 1949.

> The formulation of the common-law proscription of obscene publication did not, therefore, amount to very much. It is a good example of a social restriction that became law and was allowed to slumber until a change of social consciousness should animate. It is the prevailing social consciousness that matters quite as much as the law.[86]

In England, the contribution of Thomas Bowdler to censorship is so significant that it should be mentioned at this point. In the literary field, he is known as the prototype of an overly zealous book censor, so much so that his name has become a synonym for prudishness and senseless expurgation of good literature. Bowdlerism came into the English vocabulary after Dr. Bowdler gave up his profession as a physician and became a censor. After inheriting a fortune, he had time to follow his own desires. Shakespeare's writings provided the inspiration for his early work. He was a great admirer of the Bard as the greatest writer of England. Nevertheless, he believed that Shakespeare needed purification for the ordinary reader. He defined his task:

> ... to render the plays of Shakespeare unsullied by any scene, by any speech, or if possible, by any word that can give pain to the most chaste, or offense to the most religious of readers.[87]

---

84. *Ibid.*

85. Commonwealth v. Gordon, 66 Pa. Dist. & Co. 101 (1949).

86. Curtis Bok, "Commonwealth v. Gordon et al.," p. 101.

87. Richard Hanser, "Shakespeare, Sex ... And Dr. Bowdler," *The Saturday Review* 38 (23 April 1955): 7-8.

In 1818 he published his expurgated version, *Family Shakespeare*. Then Bowdler got out his red pencil, sharpened his scissors, and began on work on Edward Gibbon's *Decline and Fall of the Roman Empire*.

The social consciousness to which Chief Justice Bok, supra, referred, apparently brought about legislation concerning the obscenity issue in the United States. Obscenity laws were passed by Vermont in 1821, Connecticut in 1834, Massachusetts in 1835, Pennsylvania in 1860, and New York in 1868.[88]

In 1857 England passed Lord Campbell's Act. The legislation gave judges power to seize books and printed matter considered obscene. This law was the major legislative action which gave the largest impetus to the censorship of obscene materials not only in England but in America as well.[89] When Lord Campbell introduced the bill to the House of Lords, he declared it was not designed to suppress works of recognized literary or artistic merit. The act was meant to apply "exclusively to words (a) written for the single purpose of corrupting the morals of youth and (b) of a nature to shock the common feelings of decency in any well regulated mind." [90] The phrasing of the law did not make Lord Campbell's intent clear, but it did provide a clear legal definition for "obscene libel." Victorian society was ready to use Lord Campbell's Act to usher in an era of censorship.[91]

In England, the first case tried under Lord Campbell's Act was the *Hicklin*[92] case in 1868, eleven years after the English law was passed. An anti-papist pamphlet, *The Confessional Unmasked, Showing the Depravity of the Romish*

---

88. Lewis, *Literature, Obscenity, and Law*, pp. 6-7.
89. *Ibid.*, p. 7.
90. Ernst and Schwartz, *Censorship*, pp. 22-25.
91. *Ibid.*, p. 25.
92. Regina v. Hicklin, 3 L.R.-Q.B. 360 (1868).

Priesthood; the Iniquity of the Confessional, and the Questions Put to Females in Confession, was circulated and did fall into the hands of young people. This was the first major legal test for obscenity.[93] Henry Scott, author of the pamphlet and a Protestant zealot, appealed the seizure of his pamphlet to Benjamin Hicklin, Recorder of London. Hicklin ruled in favor of Scott, saying that the purpose of the pamphlet was good and not intended to corrupt. The case was sent to Justice Alexander Cockburn who reversed Hicklin's opinion on appeal.[94]

Chief Justice Cockburn delivered a verdict which became a guiding principle for judges in England and the United States:

> I think the test of obscenity is this, whether the tendency of the matter charged as obscenity is to deprave and corrupt those whose minds are open to such immoral influences, and into whose hands a publication of this sort may fall.[95]

So persuasive and impressive was Justice Cockburn's decision that its influence was felt in American courts until the middle of the twentieth century.

Thus, the scene was set in the United States, a young country with a history of interference in printed material pertaining to politics and religion. Censorship of obscenity was now added to the list. The time had arrived for the community and organized groups to become interested in purifying the reading matter of the country.

The question of appropriate reading matter for school children came into question in the South before the Civil

---

93. Ernst and Schwartz, *Censorship,* p. 35.

94. Lewis, *Literature, Obscenity, and Law,* p. 7.

95. Queen v. Hicklin, 3 L.R.-Q.B. 360 (1869), in Edward De Grazia, *Censorship Landmarks* (New York: Bowker, 1969), p. 9.

War. The South was dependent upon Northern book publishers for the majority of textbooks in the schools.
Opposing philosophies in the two regions concerning
slavery led to concern among Southern parents about the
use of certain textbooks. Geographies presented particular
anxieties since they depicted the South as inferior to the
North, discussed the evils of slavery, and stressed study of
the northern portion of the United States. The treatment of
agriculture and education as related to the Southern states
was a particular source of resentment.[96] History books were
also objectionable because of their regional bias. New
England settlers were glorified as moral patriots who
should become models for youth, while those who settled in
the South were depicted in a less favorable light.[97]

Since Northern publishers could not afford to lose the
market in the South, they began to publish modified
versions. Some published one version for the South and
another for the North, deleting objectionable passages for
the Southern version.[98]

Scientific discoveries in the early nineteenth century created conditions resulting in conflicts with religious beliefs
in both North and South. The publishing of Darwin's *Origin
of the Species* in 1859, for example, opened the door for
censorship controversies which continued into the
twentieth century.[99] One of the more famous cases, the
Scopes "monkey trial" of 1927, occurred in the southern
border state of Tennessee and it was not until 1970 that the
last state, Mississippi, finally invalidated its anti-evolution
statute.

---

96. Howard K. Beale, *A History of Freedom of Teaching in American
Schools.* Report of the Commission on the Social Studies, part XVI (New
York: Octagon Books, 1974), pp. 156-59.

97. *Ibid.,* pp. 160-62.

98. *Ibid.,* p. 164.

99. *Ibid.,* p. 202.

However, a new generation of "Genesis" statutes began to emerge in the later years decade of the 70's. The new generation of "Genesis" statutes are affectively known as "balance treatment statutes" — which required a balance treatment between teaching the scientific evolution theory and scientific creationism. Already the Federal District Court in Little Rock, with Justice William Overton writing the opinion, has declared the Arkansas "balance treatment statute" unconstitutional as First Amendment religious advance.[100] As this manuscript goes to press there are some nineteen states with similar legislative proposals.

Following the Civil War, after the ruling white class regained control in the South, protests with respect to Northern textbooks began again. The North also made demands on textbook publishers. Interest was not in unbiased textbooks. Sectional prejudice was intertwined in the subject matter of textbooks published either in the South or in those published in the North but authored by Southerners for Southern schools. Northern schools demanded publication of texts presenting the Union point of view.[101]

Moral training was a major part of the curriculum from the very beginnings of American education. Religion played an important part in the early schools. Following the Civil War, religious instruction posed problems because many religious denominations and sects existed in the country. Since no particular sect could control teaching in the schools, prohibition of teaching sectarian religious doctrine

---

100. McLean v. Arkansas Bd. of Educ., 529 F. Supp. 1955 (1982). See also Daniel v. Waters, 399 F. Supp. 510 (M.D. Tenn. 1975). In this case the Federal District Court finally validated the Tennessee "Genesis" statute lionized in *Scopes*. See also Edward C. Bolmeier's *The School in the Legal Structure* (Cincinnati: W. H. Anderson, 1973), at pp. 288-89.

101. Beale, *A History of Freedom,* p. 196.

became law in many parts of the country. Books dealing with sectarian religion were barred from classrooms and school libraries. As new state constitutions were written, public aid to parochial schools was prohibited.[102]

Barriers to teaching sectarian religion were not intended to eliminate religion from schools. They were intended to permit Bible reading and the teaching of non-sectarian Protestantism in the public schools. "Men were as eager to protect children against no religion as against sectarian proselyting." [103]

In 1875 President Ulysses S. Grant proposed a federal constitutional amendment forbidding the teaching of religious tenets in school and prohibiting the use of school funds or school taxes for the benefit of any religious denomination or sect.[104] Even though such an amendment was never adopted until 1903, thirty-nine states had passed legislation prohibiting the teaching of sectarian religion in the public schools.[105] The issue continued into the twentieth century.

Following the Civil War, Anthony Comstock moved from Connecticut to New York. He began his career as a dry goods clerk and then as a salesman. At the age of eighteen he was a crusader against the evils of liquor. His real interest, however, was in prevention of the moral decay of the country. In 1866 the New York YMCA made a survey of vile and licentious books, magazines, and newspapers for sale in New York. The survey found New York filled with such publications. The YMCA urged the the state legislature to pass a bill to suppress these publications.[106]

---

102. *Ibid.*, pp. 208-09.
103. *Ibid.*, p. 210.
104. *Ibid.*, p. 209.
105. *Ibid.*
106. Ernst and Schwartz, *Censorship*, pp. 30-33.

Comstock read about the survey and ensuing action. He had found his cause. He became a crusader, a self-appointed censor. With the help of a wealthy friend, Morris K. Jessup, he became a leader of the censorship movement in New York. Jessup was president of the YMCA and founder of the American Museum of Natural History. Together the two men founded the New York Society for the Suppression of Vice, which was designed to rid the city of moral decay and to protect the young and innocent. Comstock became its secretary in 1873, and was given power to make arrests in the name of decency. He was made a special agent of the Post Office. In that role he lobbied for a stronger Federal Obscenity Bill. He helped form the New England Society for the Suppression of Vice.[107] The Federal Obscenity Bill passed and other states throughout the nation were led to enact similar laws. The Midwest formed a similar society and Boston fostered the New England Watch and Ward Society.[108]

The term "comstockery" became a synonym for the crusading censor just as "Bowdlerism" had in England. Thus, Anthony Comstock took his place in history. The laws passed under his tutelage are still known as Comstock Laws.[109]

Many librarians in the nineteenth century were influenced by various vice societies. "Harmless" literature was the type selected for the shelves of numerous libraries. Adventurous and improbable literature was criticized because it gave false notions about life. Different collections were kept in the main library as compared with those at the branches. Those who wanted "immoral" classics had to go to the main library to obtain them. Factory workers usually

---

107. Davis, *Dealing with Censorship*, p. ix.
108. *Ibid.*
109. Haney, *Comstockery in America*, p. 6.

read books at branch libraries where "dangerous" literature was not available.[110]

Even when best sellers (the main targets for attack) were available in libraries, librarians had methods for seeing that they were circulated only to certain readers. Books by foreign authors such as Emil Zola, Rabelais, Boccaccio, and Paul de Kock were sometimes purchased only in the native language of the authors. The books were loaned exclusively to scholars and highly educated persons.[111]

Frequently, reference collections contained the type of books ordinarily available in present day collections of fiction. Librarians restricted their use to students and scholars, thus protecting youth and the common man from improper reading. Many librarians thus were actually censors of books and "protectors" of the populace from improper reading in the nineteenth century.[112]

Twentieth Century.

The turn of the century brought with it many social and economic problems as the United States moved from an agrarian economy to an industrialized nation. Public schools in America were in the process of change. By the end of World War I, teacher training had improved to the point that public school teachers were capable of demanding more freedom in their roles than ever before. Knowledge in science was expanding rapidly. Higher education institutions were requiring that teachers' preparation include more history, civics, economics, and sociology as well as sciences.[113]

---

110. Evelyn Geller, "The Librarian as Censor," *Library Journal* 101 (June 1976): 1255-58.

111. *Ibid.*

112. *Ibid.*

113. Beale, *A History of Freedom,* pp. 227-39.

The public developed a new and stronger patriotism as a result of the "war to end all wars." Patriotic societies and pressure groups began to spring up to support many causes.[114]

Moreover censorship was still a judicial problem in America with twelve landmark cases coming from the courts between 1908 and 1929.[115] Public schools began to feel pressures within the community as well as from various groups concerning curricular matters and the materials used in teaching children. More literature was available for children and young people than ever before. For this reason, emphasis on review of the censorship literature in this section of the study will concern: (a) literature for children in the public schools; and (b) the influence of public involvement and pressure groups in the affairs of the schools.

The reformers who ushered in the Progressive Age of the early 1900s wanted to ameliorate the human misery indigenous to poverty and squalor in an urban environment. In the early stages of the movement, the vice societies which had developed in the late 1800s were welcomed under the progressive tent. If obscene reading matter was a vice which needed to be removed to improve social conditions, then the reformers supported removal. Later social reformers dropped the cause of censorship when they adopted statistical surveys and other investigative procedures. The effects of reading obscenity were difficult to prove by the new investigative approach.[116]

The early Progressive reformers, however, found documentation for their fears. The first annual report of the

---

114. *Ibid.*

115. De Grazia, *Censorship Landmarks*, pp. v-vi.

116. Paul S. Boyer, *Purity in Print: The Vice Society Movement and Book Censorship in America* (New York: Charles Scribner, 1968), pp. 23-27. See also Lawrence A. Cremin, *The Transformation of the School* (New York: Alfred A. Knoft, 1961), pp. 58-90.

American Social Hygiene Association urged teachers and parents to inspire "the soul with the highest religious and family and civic ideal."[117] In so doing, the minds of the young could, hopefully, be diverted from thoughts of the obscene.[118] The probation officers of the juvenile courts of Chicago reported that many delinquent girls had been corrupted by evil literature.[119] The prominent psychologist, G. Stanley Hall, called for protection of youth from erotic reading material in his book, *Adolescence,* published in 1904.[120]

In 1903 the Brooklyn Public Library removed *Tom Sawyer* and *Huckleberry Finn* from the children's collection. Samuel Clemens stated in defense that he had written the two books for adults and was distressed whenever he heard that they were available to children. Mrs. Clemens then censored *Huckleberry Finn* by deleting profanity and many other passages. The language used in the books was the problem.[121] Non-standard English was a current concern of parents as it is today. *Huckleberry Finn* continues to draw criticism in the public schools because of the use of the term "nigger." [122]

In 1911 a committee of Jews and Gentiles asked school officials in Meriden, Connecticut, to remove *The Merchant of Venice* from the study of Shakespeare in the public schools. The committee believed that Shylock, the Jewish usurer in the play, presented a false stereotype and tended to create hatred against Jewish people. The wishes of the committee were granted.[123]

---

117. "Progress, 1900-1915," *Social Hygiene,* 11 (January 1916): 40.

118. *Ibid.,* pp. 37-47.

119. Boyer, *Purity in Print,* p. 27.

120. *Ibid.*

121. Haight, *Banned Books,* p. 57.

122. Haney, *Comstockery in America,* p. 158.

123. Jack Nelson and Gene Roberts, Jr., *Censors and the Schools* (Boston: Little, Brown and Company, 1963), p. 4.

Sex education in the schools has been, and still is, an inflammatory issue among parents and pressure groups. Many children in 1919 were receiving sex education from companions rather than from parents, the church, or the school. Mary Ware Dennett wrote a pamphlet for the instruction of her own two sons. Rather than using the birds and bees as analogy, she wrote a frank pamphlet on human sexuality. Several religious and educational institutions were so impressed with her work that it was printed for distribution among their organizations.

In 1926 a Mrs. Miles from Virginia received through the mail a copy from the author. Mrs. Miles was an entrapper for the Post Office Department and reported the receipt of the pamphlet. The Post Office charged Mrs. Dennett with violation of the Comstock mail law. She was tried by a judge and jury, convicted, and fined $300. Mrs. Dennett "told the judge that if in fact she had corrupted youth, $300 would be too light a penalty, and that she would go to jail if the conviction were sustained on appeal." [124]

The judge insisted the jury was not mistaken in the facts. But alas, he decided the case should have never been presented to a jury. Finally, the judge maintained the pamphlet was not obscene and therefore could not be a violation of the Federal Obscenity Law.

During the 1920s all librarians were not crusaders against censorship, nor was the American Civil Liberties Union. At the same time, liberal weeklies such as *Nation* and *New Republic* were spokesmen against censorship. As a result, both publications were banned from school libraries in Los Angeles in 1921.[125]

In the same year, the United States Commissioner of Education banned the teaching of communism and

---

124. Ernst and Schwartz, *Censorship*, p. 81.
125. Blanshard, *The Right to Read*, p. 90.

socialism from schools. The Lusk committee of New York legislature recommended that any teacher who did not approve of the American social system should give up his teaching position.[126]

During the era of the 1920s, public utility companies decided textbooks should be rewritten so children would learn to appreciate the private enterprise system. Under the involved leadership of Samuel Insull, utilities officials formed a special committee to censor school books bearing on the utility situation. The Federal Trade Commission investigated, but by that time many textbooks had been removed from the schools or had been changed to meet the philosophy of the utility companies.[127]

Two patriotic organizations that became involved in criticism of textbooks following World War I were the American Legion and the Veterans of Foreign Wars. The American Legion did not believe history textbooks instilled enough patriotism in students. Since no textbook could be found to satisfy their requirements, the Legion commissioned the writing of such a book in 1922.[128]

The Veterans of Foreign Wars were interested in eliminating un-American textbooks from public schools. The National Americanization Committee was formed for that purpose. By the late 1920s the Committee announced that their goal had been accomplished and they were now ready to concern themselves with modern European history texts.[129]

Members of the American Historical Association were offended by the post World-War-I groups who called history texts un-American. They expressed dissatisfaction by

---

126. *Ibid.*
127. *Ibid.*, pp. 90-91.
128. Nelson and Roberts, *Censors and the Schools*, p. 28.
129. *Ibid.*

protesting that such accusations implied historians were involved in the writing of treason. Such accusations, insisted the historical association, were absurd. Their protests did not stop pressure from various groups.[130]

Many pressure groups aimed their anger at England, our wartime ally. Charles Grant Miller wrote a series of articles for the Hearst newspapers warning parents against "Anglicized" history textbooks.[131] He examined the books and expressed his wrath when a figure from history "he disliked received more attention than one he admired."[132] Mayor John F. Hylan, of New York, hired Miller to carry out a textbook investigation.[133]

Mayor William Hart Thompson of Chicago launched a series of attacks on history textbooks in his re-election campaign in 1927 and 1928. Many of his charges were ridiculous since he claimed the King of England had "persuaded Chicago's Superintendent of Schools to remove George Washington's picture from the books." [134]

Attacks on textbooks in the 1920s led to legislation in various states. Oregon, Wisconsin, and Oklahoma passed bills stating that educators must select no book speaking slightingly of the founders of our nation or the men who preserved the union. Textbook investigations took place in many cities and towns throughout the country.[135]

Harold Rugg, Professor Emeritus of Education, Columbia University, published a series of social science textbooks widely used during the depression era. His books raised questions that had not been mentioned previously in school

---

130. *Ibid.*, p. 23.
131. *Ibid.*, p. 27.
132. *Ibid.*
133. *Ibid.*
134. *Ibid.*, p. 28.
135. *Ibid.*, p. 29.

textbooks. Professor Rugg believed that teachers and the public had been awakened to social and economic problems of the nation during the depression.[136] He "suggested that society should be studied as a rapidly changing phenomenon to be reshaped from generation to generation according to changing standards of value." [137]

From 1938 to 1942 the greatest pressure group campaign ever staged against a textbook author was waged against Professor Rugg. Conservative business groups supplied money and research while the American Legion led the publicity. The National Association of Manufacturers joined the campaign. The American Legion made a list of un-American textbooks and literature in the schools and recommended that they be removed from the schools.[138]

Mrs. Elmwood J. Turner, corresponding secretary of the Daughters of Colonial Wars, wrote of Professor Rugg in 1940 that he

> tried to give the child an unbiased viewpoint instead of teaching him real Americanism. All the old historians taught: "My country right or wrong." That's the point of view we want our children to adopt. We can't afford to teach them to be unbiased and let them make up their own minds.[139]

Some school systems gave in to the pressure. Others continued to use the textbooks until they became worn and out of date. Professor Rugg made a statement to the self-appointed censors:

> Censor the schools and you convict yourselves by your very acts as the most subversive enemies of democracy. Censor education and you destroy understanding . . .

---

136. Beale, *A History of Freedom*, pp. 270-71.

137. Blanshard, *The Right to Read*, p. 92.

138. *Ibid.*, pp. 92-94.

139. *Ibid.*, pp. 95-96.

you instate bias . . . you give free reign to prejudice . . . finally, you create fascism. Nothing but an education in the whole of American life will build tolerant understanding of our people and guarantee the perpetuation of democracy.[140]

In 1948 *The Nation* was banned from an official list of accepted periodicals approved for high schools in New York City. This act of censorship was the result of a series of articles that appeared in *The Nation* between November 1, 1947, and June 5, 1948. Paul Blanshard was the author of the articles which concerned the Roman Catholic Church.[141]

There had been no protests from the Catholic Church. The Superintendent of Schools explained his action in a statement entitled, "Should Religious Beliefs Be Studied and Criticized in an American Public High School?"[142] A temporary committee composed of seventy-two well-known individuals representing thirty-four organizations was appointed. Archibald MacLeish led the opposition. *The Nation* was eventually restored to the New York high schools.

Censorship was not a major issue for public schools in the early 1950s although some instances did occur. *The Newsletter on Intellectual Freedom* of the American Library Association cited some of those that did happen.

Mrs. Myrtle G. Hance of Texas headed a group called Minute Women of America that published a list entitled,

---

140. Harold Rugg, "A Study in Censorship: Good Concepts and Bad Words," in *The First Freedom*, ed. Robert B. Downs (Chicago: American Library Association, 1960), p. 349.

141. Archibald W. Anderson, "'The Nation' Cause," in *The First Freedom*, ed. Robert B. Downs (Chicago: American Library Association, 1960), pp. 353-59.

142. *Ibid.*, p. 354.

"What to Look for in the Library of Your School." First on that list was *A Field of Broken Stones,* by Lowel Naeve and David Wieck. The list stated that the book was filthy, immoral, and politically dangerous.[143]

The thirty-year period from 1950 through 1980 brought about many changes in American society and public schools. The federal government's grants and aid to public schools required schools to follow specific guidelines and meet specific criteria which influenced curricula. There was a renewal of interest in science instruction following the Russian launching of Sputnik. The civil rights movement, the Supreme Court order to desegregate public schools, the war in Vietnam, changing life-styles, the women's movement, and laws concerning the education of handicapped children led to public school involvement in litigation and public unrest. A new religious revival made the presence or absence of religious books in the public schools a sensitive subject. The Watergate investigation, high taxes, and inflation led to public cynicism toward government which, in turn, led to attacks on the public schools.

In the early 1950s the Conference of American Small Business Organizations published *Educational Reviewer*, issued quarterly to evaluate educational materials. The publication issued the results of its examination of textbooks as they related to personal and economic liberty and "concealed theories of collectivism." [144] The United States House of Representatives Select Committee on Lobbying Activities investigated the activities of the organization. The committee report concluded:

> We all agree, of course, that our textbooks should be American, that they should not be the vehicle for the propagation of obnoxious doctrines. Yet the review of

---

143. *Newsletter on Intellectual Freedom* 3 (January 25, 1955): 3.
144. Rugg, "A Study in Censorship," p. 343.

textbooks by self-appointed experts, especially when undertaken under the aegis of an organization having a distinct legislative ax to grind, smacks too much of the book-burning orgies of Nuremberg to be accepted by thoughtful Americans without foreboding and alarm. It suggests, too that the reviewers distrust the integrity, good faith, and plain common sense of the school boards and teachers of the country. If these educators are so utterly naive and untrained as to need help from a lobbying organization in selecting proper classroom materials, then our educational system has decayed beyond all help. This proposition we cannot accept.[145]

During the McCarthy era, schools found themselves under attack sometimes in a ridiculous manner. In 1953, Mrs. Thomas J. White was a member of the Indiana Textbook Commission. She determined that *Robin Hood* was communistic and should be removed from the Indiana schools. She further expressed the opinion that any reference to the Quaker religion be eliminated from textbooks. She felt that since Quakers did not believe in fighting wars, they helped Communism.[146] Mrs. White lost her fight against these two areas.

Following World War II, critics looked at textbooks for any remark favorable to the Soviet Union. The decade of the fifties was one of action. In at least one instance action was extreme. In 1953 Alabama passed a law forbidding the use of any textbook or other written instructional materials (except newspapers and magazines) unless the publisher or author stated that no author involved in the book was a member of any Communist group or a Marxist socialist. State public schools, trade schools, and institutions of higher learning were included. Book publishers, authors,

---

145. *Ibid.*, p. 344.
146. Blanshard, *Right to Read*, pp. 83-84.

the Alabama Education Association, and nine Alabama college presidents went to court over the issue. The court declared the law null and void under the due process clause of the Fourteenth Amendment.[147]

In 1957 it was reported that the Texas unit of pro-America reviewed each textbook in the state so that political ideas conflicting with the United States Constitution were not presented in the schools.[148] In February of that year the Associate Superintendent of the Philadelphia Schools stated that the Daughters of the American Revolution had the Board of Education's approval to inspect textbooks for subversive materials. He insisted that their evaluations would be taken seriously.[149]

In March, 1957, a newly elected school board member in Houston, Texas, objected to a tenth-grade geography book that taught "United Nations propaganda and one-worldism." She also objected to ideologies in a twelfth-grade economics book. The Superintendent resigned in digust.[150]

In Nebraska the Daughters of the American Revolution, because of the organization's objections to policies of the United Nations, asked that state educational institutions stop using any educational materials put out by the United Nations Educational, Scientific, and Cultural Organization. In 1958 the National Association of Secondary School Principals at their convention, declared that *Life* and *Time* magazines were not favorable to education. The Association sent notices to nearly twenty thousand principals sug-

---

147. Renick C. Kennedy, "Alabama Book Toasters," in *The First Freedom,* ed. Robert B. Downs (Chicago: American Library Association, 1960), pp. 375-77.

148. *Newsletters on Intellectual Freedom* 6 (March, 1957): 7.

149. *Ibid.*

150. *Ibid.*, 6 (June, 1957): 9.

gesting that they question the circulation of these magazines.[151]

In the 1960s schools began to change. Financed in part by federal funds fostering change and innovation—open classrooms, team teaching, individualized instruction, new mathematics, and alternative curricula entered the public schools of the United States. To many parents this change brought confusion. The traditional classroom which most parents had attended had almost disappeared from the public schools. Parents could not understand their children's homework especially in mathematics. Educational emphasis moved from teaching facts to understanding concepts. Decision making, thinking skills, and values clarification were part of the curriculum. In many cases, students decided what they wanted to learn, when, and how. Parents began to wonder whether their children were learning.[152]

At about the same time, literature for children and young people began to change as well. Realistic literature, based on the changes in society, began to be published. Former literature patterns, designed to be uplifting and to free the imagination of the child (the books read by parents), were changing with the times. Young readers, whose life styles differed from those of their parents, had different interests. Authors began writing books about the new life styles that interested youth. Personal and social problems often became the theme of the new books.

The new realism in literature for young people and children explored topics formerly reserved for adult literature.

---

151. *Ibid.*, 7 (June, 1958): 6.

152. Jon Schaffarzick, "Federal Curriculum Reform: A Crucible for Value Conflicts," in *Value Conflicts and Curriculum Issues: Lessons from Research and Experience,* eds. Jon Schaffarzick and Gary Sykes (Berkley: McCutchan, 1979), pp. 1-24.

Themes for the new realism are described in an article in *Phi Delta Kappan.*[153]

The first theme covered in many children's books is changing family patterns. This theme includes topics such as one-parent households, divorce, estranged parents, foster-home living, working mothers, living on welfare, parental dating, and problems faced by families who move from place to place.[154]

A second theme seldom covered earlier in children's literature is death and dying. Whereas books written previously might cover the death of a pet, the new books cover the loss of grandparents, parents, siblings, and friends. Death is presented as an actual experience that everyone must face at one time or another.[155]

A third major theme is that of a variety of ethnic groups living in our pluralistic society. "As we grow in our realization that we are a pluralistic society, that our strengths and accomplishments flow from the diversity of our people, these books represent a new honesty."[156] Children living in geographic areas lacking a diversity of ethnic groups can learn about different people through the books. The use of nonstandard English in some of the books often brought parental criticism.

A fourth theme deals with changing roles of males and females. *Free to be You and Me* by Marlo Thomas explores possibilities for both boys and girls in their futures. This type of book looks at changing patterns in careers as well as in life styles.[157]

---

153. Lee Rinsky and Roman Schweikert, "In Defense of the 'New Realism' for Children and Adolescents," *Phi Delta Kappan* 58 (February, 1977): 472-75.

154. *Ibid.*, p. 473.

155. *Ibid.*

156. *Ibid.*

157. *Ibid.*, p. 474.

Fiction covers not only the themes listed above, but also topics formerly taboo in books for children and adolescents. Adolescent physical change, pregnancy, abortion, homosexuality, birth, and the use of drugs and alcohol are treated with equal honesty.[158]

Within all of these themes will be found good and bad books. Many of them use street language; some books use this device effectively and without a design for shock. Others apparently use mature themes and language for shock value, rather than treating themes with human dignity, in order to sell the product.[159]

School boards, administrators, librarians, and teachers are faced with a tremendous responsibility as a result of the new literature for young people. Schools are sensitive to public pressure. Children like the new themes. The market is flooded with good and poor literature. Schools are responsible for a balanced collection that meets the needs of the school curriculum and satisfies the reading interests of the children of the school. Many English teachers teach modern literature that appeals to students.[160]

Librarians, teachers, and school administrators are faced with the responsibility of preparing students for a real world filled with social change. At the same time school administrators and teachers need community support in accomplishing education goals. Censorship attempts and controversy have increased as social change and new themes in literature have developed.[161]

Professionals in the field of education take different positions on the selection of literature and instructional mate-

---

158. *Ibid.*

159. *Ibid.*

160. Ann Kalkhoff, "Innocent Children or Innocent Librarians" in *Issues in Children's Book Selection: A School Library Journal/Library Journal Anthology* (New York: R. R. Bowker, 1973), pp. 11-19.

161. Jenkinson, "Dirty Dictionaries," pp. 7-11.

rials. These positions range from: (1) those who think any type of censorship is wrong; (2) those who believe that good selection based on community standards is necessary; and (3) those who fear to select any controversial material. Most educators and librarians educational philosophy range at some point along this spectrum. Positions vary according to materials involved and current educational climate.

Publishers and authors have been caught up in the controversy. While the literature described above can be a valuable tool for teaching about our changing world, authors and publishers are warned that traditional books must also be available to students. The pendulum must not swing too far.[162]

Publishers are, of necessity, cognizant of the work of censors. They cannot afford to lose an educational market through knowingly antagonizing an active censorship group. James J. O'Donnell, Executive Editor of Xerox Educational Publications, made the following statement,

> After all, a single hardback, four color series can represent a million-dollar investment. So when Texas, or California, or some other large state or city sets its terms, the publishers take heed.[163]

Mr. O'Donnell asked that educators maintain an honest and competent environment in selection and that successful censorship attempts come only from highly qualified and courageous censors.[164] Publishers have listened to public

---

162. Jo M. Stanchfield, "Trends—Not Destiny," in *Indoctrinate or Educate?* eds. Thomas C. Hatcher and Lawrence G. Erickson (Newark, Del.: International Reading Association, 1979), p. 21.
163. James J. O'Donnell, "Censorship and the Publishers," *NASSP Bulletin* 59 (May, 1975): 59-63.
164. *Ibid.*, p. 63.

pressure toward conservatism. Some publishers have begun modifying the content of textbooks.[165]

Judy Blume is an author of books on many of the above stated themes. Her books are among the most popular with young people and are the subject of recent attacks.[166] In 1977 an article entitled "Old Values Surface in Blume Country"[167] attacked the author's works as "racist, sexist, elite, or any combination of the three." In an interview responding to the criticism,[168] Ms. Blume stated that the Council on Interracial Books for Children that published the article is trying to tell her and other authors what to write and how to write in the future. When asked whether there is value in telling young people how to act and what to do in books, she responded:

> kids don't buy preaching and being preached to. There's more value in presenting *real* situations and real characters even if they aren't pretty. I love to see a movie or a play and then go home and think about it, to draw my own conclusions about it. In the same way, I want kids to read my books and think about them and draw their own conclusions about human nature and the human condition.[169]

Censorship has increased in the twenty-two-year period from 1960 through 1982. The cause may be related to reaction to societal change, new realism in literature, governmental interference in many sectors of private lives,

---

165. Pham Thein Hung, "Parents Protest Textbooks," *Freedom of Information Center Report No. 401* (Columbia, Mo.: School of Journalism, University of Missouri, March, 1979), p. 10.

166. Rinsky and Schwikert, "In Defense of the 'New Realism,' " p. 474.

167. "Old Values Surface in Blume Country." *Bulletin of the Council on Interracial Books for Children* 7 (1977): 8-10.

168. "Some 'Isms' Revisited, Answers from Blume Country: An Interview with Judy Blume," *Top of the News* 34 (Spring, 1978): 233-43.

169. *Ibid.*, p. 235.

changing patterns in education, and lack of public confidence in education.

An examination of what has been censored in public schools shows the enormity of the situation. Representative cases are cited as published in the *Newsletter on Intellectual Freedom.*[170]

In December, 1960, the National Association for the Advancement of Colored People banned an English textbook from the high school at Torrington, Connecticut. The textbook contained stories that embarrassed Negro students: Edgar Allen Poe's *Gold Bug,* Joel Chandler Harris's *Br'er Rabbit,* and *Sonny's Christening* by Ruth Stuart. The *New York Herald Tribune* wrote that in spite of sympathy for Negro children, education would be in a sad state if only inoffensive literature were taught.[171]

In 1961 a Church of Christ minister, a member of the Committee for Fundamental Education, objected to use of forty books in the Bolsa Grand High School in Garden Grove, California.[172]

Also, in 1961 the John Birch Society leader, Rogert W. Welch, Jr., told reporters anti-Communist textbooks were needed in schools. All others should be removed. He urged people sympathetic with this cause to take over the Parent-Teacher Associations to accomplish this purpose.[173]

During the same year a parent in Santa Ana, California objected to the playing of a record of Archibald MacLeish's *J.B.* in the classroom. The same parent also objected to *Catcher in the Rye* by J.D. Salinger and any book by George Bernard Shaw and Tennessee Williams.[174]

---

170. 10 (March, 1961): 3.
171. *Ibid.*
172. *Ibid.*, p. 7.
173. *Ibid.*, p. 3.
174. *Ibid.*, p. 4.

In 1962 a high school teacher in Wrenshall, Minnesota was fired for teaching George Orwell's *1984*. The teacher later regained his job. In the same year parents attempted to ban John Steinbeck's *The Grapes of Wrath* from a high school in Tacoma, Washington. The school board stopped the banning.[175]

In 1962 Texans for America supported by the John Birch Society, American Legion, and Daughters of the American Revolution, put pressure concerning textbooks on the Texas legislature. The legislature appointed an examining committee of five. Their task was to remove from Texas schools any books favorable to the New Deal, United Nations, Tennessee Valley Authority, or federal aid to almost anything. They were also to rid Texas schools of books describing the United States as a democracy rather than a republic, and any books with selections by Pete Seeger and Langston Hughes because of past Communist affiliation. Also to be removed were books containing the name of Albert Einstein, music books with Jewish songs, and a long list of books such as John Steinbeck's *The Grapes of Wrath*, Alfred B. Guthrie, Jr.'s *Big Sky*, Aldous Huxley's *Brave New World*, McKinley Kantor's *Andersonville*, Thomas Wolfe's *Of Time and the River*, and George Orwell's *1984*. Needless to say, the committee was unable to accomplish the task completely.[176]

In 1970 the principal of Jordan Junior High School in Minneapolis restricted Eve Merriam's *Inner City Mother Goose* to use by faculty only. The Facts Committee for Equal Education said the book was obscene and advocated violence. This group was part of the Neighborhood School Committee which opposed mandatory busing.[177]

---

175. *Ibid.*, p. 1.
176. *Newsletter on Intellectual Freedom* 11 (July, 1962): 4-5.
177. *Ibid.*, 20 (January, 1971): 4.

In November, 1971, William Steig's *Sylvester and the Magic Pebble* was removed from the shelves of the Toledo public school libraries pending review. This children's animal story had policemen pictured as pigs.[178]

In 1971 the Strongville, Ohio school board announced that they would review all textbooks for obscenities, immorality, and abuse of the deity of God. They also planned to look into whether matters presented in books were depressing or inspirational toward historical figures and to look at presentations concerning economics and politics of the country.[179]

In 1971 a parent at Holmes Junior High School in Cedar Rapids, Iowa, objected to two books highly recommended by *School Library Journal*. The superintendent announced that school librarians would screen books more carefully in the future.[180]

Citizens in Kalamazoo, Michigan, in 1971 asked for the removal of Joan Baez' autobiography, *Daybreak*. The American Civil Liberties Union came to the defense of the book, saying that no self-appointed censors should decide what was to remain in the school library.[181]

In 1971 in Stayton, Oregon, there was a controversy over books in the school library. A screening committee of concerned parents was appointed because parents are taxpayers and should be involved. The committee threw away anything questionable in paperback editions after glancing at them. They discarded any book with love scenes and/or dirty language and blacked out many passages.[182]

In Clay County, Georgia, in 1971 an English teacher who

---

178. *Ibid.*, p. 5.
179. *Ibid.*, 20 (March, 1971): 32-33.
180. *Ibid.*, p. 60.
181. *Ibid.*, p. 61.
182. *Ibid.*, p. 123.

had been fired was reinstated and paid five thousand dollars in damages. He was fired for using an article from *Playboy* and showing a surrealistic movie by Salvador Dali in the classroom.[183]

In Buncombe County, North Carolina, in 1973, a school board member, Mrs. Edna Roberts, removed *Catcher in the Rye,* by J. D. Salinger, *Of Mice and Men* by John Steinbeck, *Andersonville* by McKinley Kantor, and *Learning Tree* by Gordon Parks, from the high school library. She demanded that all books containing "objectionable" words be removed from school libraries. After a long battle, Mrs. Roberts lost her struggle and books were replaced on the shelves.[184]

In 1975 pressure from the Concerned Parents Committee in Randolph, New York, brought about the removal of nearly 150 books from the high school library. The books were locked in a safe until a screening committee could make a decision on their appropriateness for high school students.[185]

In the same year, books were removed from the library shelves in Scituate, Rhode Island, and Waukesha, Wisconsin. Peter Benchley's *Jaws,* Peter Gent's *North Dallas Forty,* and *Go Ask Alice* were removed from the shelves of a Dallas, Texas, high school library. All removals were brought about by pressure from parents.[186]

In 1976 pressure from a school board member, a Baptist minister, caused the removal of James Fenimore Cooper's *Drums Along the Mohawk* from a required reading list in Manchester, Tennessee. The book was banned because it contains the words "hell" and "damn." [187]

---

183. *Ibid.,* p. 130.

184. *Ibid.,* 22 (May, 1973): 52.

185. *Ibid.,* 24 (July, 1975): 103.

186. *Ibid.*

187. *Ibid.,* 25 (November, 1976): 145.

In the fall of 1978 a Thatcher, Arizona, high school librarian found all but four periodicals had been removed from the library over the summer. One thousand and one hundred volumes, involving sixty-five titles, had disappeared. No reason was given. A school board committee told her they would study the matter.[188]

In 1978 in Helena, Montana, a member of Phyllis Schlafly's Eagle Forum borrowed and refused to return the book *Our Bodies, Ourselves,* by the Women's Health Collective. The school district trustees removed all copies from all school libraries.[189]

The cases cited above are only a few of many that were reported by the *Newsletter on Intellectual Freedom* during the years from 1960 through 1978. Many cases were resolved without publicity during this period. Others which reached the courts will be reported in the following chapter.

Recent surveys indicate that censorship has been on the rise in public schools throughout the nation. As indicated in Chapter 1, more accounts were received in 1977 and 1978 than in the previous twenty-five years.[190]

A survey conducted by the Intellectual Freedom Committee of the North Carolina Library Association had responses from 592 librarians. Although librarians from public, college, university, junior college, and public schools were surveyed, only responses from public school librarians will be discussed. Responses from school librarians determined that 53.8 percent had avoided purchasing material because of anticipated censorship problems, 44.7 percent had not avoided purchase, 1.5 percent failed to respond to the question.[191]

---

188. *Ibid.,* 27 (November, 1978): 138.

189. *Ibid.*

190. "Textbook Censors: You Can Survive Their Ire and Extinguish Their Fire," p. 26.

191. Unpublished survey of the Intellectual Freedom Committee of

Ninety public school librarians, or 15.2 percent, reported they had received complaints which required formal action by the governing body of the library. Three hundred nineteen, or 53.8 percent, responded that they had faced censorship problems of some type. In answer to a question about whether the school had written selection policies, 84.3 percent reported they had formal written policies, 11.5 percent had no written selection policy, 3.5 percent did not know, and 0.7 percent did not answer.

What were the grounds for complaints in the North Carolina schools? Profanity was the number one indication with 72 complaints, or 40.2 percent; sex was second with 62 complaints, or 34.6 percent; religion ranked third with 18 complaints, or 10.1 percent; race ranked fourth with 8 complaints, or 4.5 percent; violence was fifth with 5 complaints, or 2.8 percent; and the last category was listed as "other" with 14 complaints, or 7.8 percent.[192]

Three hundred eighty-six educators were surveyed in the fall of 1974 by Curriculum Information Network, sponsored jointly by Social Education and the Social Science Education Consortium. The survey focused on controversy concerning materials and topics in education. This review concerns only reports involving materials. There were no previous comparable studies for comparison on controversial issues and their treatment.[193]

One hundred forty-seven controversial issues involving materials were classified under ten categories. Of the ten categories, sex and sex education tied with school operations for the top issue. Content and context, unspecified by

---

the North Carolina Library Association, April, 1979. Conducted by Phil Morris and Martha E. Davis. (Typewritten.)

192. *Ibid.*

193. Irving Morrissett, "Curriculum Network Fourth Report: Controversies in the Classroom," *Social Education* 39 (April, 1975): 246-52.

the survey, ranked second. Other social issues third, and religious and philosophical issues ranked fourth. Objectionable language and political issues tied for fifth place, and racial issues ranked sixth in the survey.

The respondents were asked how well the controversies concerning materials were resolved. The results showed that six were resolved creatively and amicably, seventy-four satisfactorily, twenty-five only partially, and twenty-six were not resolved.[194]

The Curriculum Information Network Survey cannot be said to be representative of the nation since the sample was small and since it represented only those who are involved in a subject area as sensitive as social studies. The survey however, does establish that controversy exists in the social science areas of the school program.

Lemuel Byrd Woods' extensive study on censorship of educational institutions in the United States from 1966 to 1977 provides additional information.[195] Dr. Woods' study included public libraries as well as public school libraries. The following table has been drawn from his work to illustrate what happened in public schools during the ten-year period. The column marked K-12 covered public school cases that did not indicate the level where the book was censored.[196]

---

194. *Ibid.*, p. 249.

195. L. B. Woods, *A Decade of Censorship in America: The Threat to Classrooms and Libraries,* 1966-1975 (Metuchen, New Jersey: Scarecrow Press, 1979).

196. *Ibid.*, p. 73.

TABLE 1

TYPES OF MATERIALS CENSORED IN SCHOOLS
IN THE UNITED STATES
1966-1975

	High School	Junior High	Elemen-tary	K-12	Total
Art Works	1			3	4
Booklets			1		· 1
Books	767	61	222	13	1,063
Films	11	2	2	3	18
Filmstrips	1				1
Handouts	1				1
Magazines	18	5	3	11	37
Newspapers	71	1	1	5	78
Poems	2		1		3
Recordings		1	1	1	3
Slide Shows	1			1	2
Textbooks	88	29	6	176	299
Totals	961	99	237	213	1,510

SOURCE: L. B. Woods, *A Decade of Censorship in America: The Threat to Classroom and Libraries, 1966-1975* (Metuchen, New Jersey: Scarecrow Press, 1979), p. 60.

Dr. Woods indicated that the number of cases reported doubled in the 1970s. He stated that this may be due to: (1) better reporting procedures by the *Newsletter on Intellectual Freedom* where he collected data; (2) more reports from librarians because they were more alert toward censorship; and (3) an actual rise in censorship attempts "as people became more aware and sensitive to materials they considered offensive." [197]

---

197. *Ibid.*, pp. 144-45.

During the years 1970, 1974, and 1975, 114 cases were reported each year. Twenty-seven cases were reported in 1966. Seventy-three cases were reported in 1967, an increase of 172.2 percent.[198]

The District of Columbia and Rhode Island had the heaviest censorship activity between 1966 and 1975. Other areas with heavy censorship were Vermont, New Hampshire, Maryland, Virginia (in the area adjacent to the District of Columbia), Oregon, Montana, and Wyoming. It must be remembered that these statistics cover other libraries as well as those in schools.[199]

Books accounted for the most censorship attempts.[200] Schools were the main target, receiving 62 percent more censorship attempts than did other educational institutions.[201] *Catcher in the Rye* was the most censored book in the United States.[202]

Among the most active organizations at work in the United States questioning school instructional materials since 1961 has been Educational Research Analysts, Inc. This non-profit, tax-exempt enterprise is headed by Mel and Norma Gabler who operate from their home in Longview, Texas. Their stated goal is to help parents through evaluation of textbooks, library books, and instructional materials used by schools in the United States, Canada, Australia, and New Zealand. The Gablers refer to their organization as the "nation's largest textbook clearinghouse." They deny being censors.[203]

---

198. *Ibid.*, p. 145.

199. *Ibid.*, pp. 145-46.

200. *Ibid.*, p. 147.

201. *Ibid.*, p. 148.

202. *Ibid.*, p. 149.

203. Barbara Parker, "Your Schools May Be the Next Battlefield in the Crusade Against 'Improper' Textbooks," *American School Board Journal* 166 (June, 1979): 27.

The Gablers indicate they spend many hours poring over each detail of the books they evaluate. In addition, they send outlines to interested parents who want to participate in the operation. Ten categories are suggested to parents as they look for objectionable content:

> (1) Attacks on Values, (2) Distorted Content, (3) Negative Thinking, (4) Violence, (5) Academic Unexcellence, (6) Isms Fostered (Communism, Socialism, Internationalism), (7) Invasion of Privacy, (8) Behavioral Modification, (9) Humanism, Occult, and Other Religions Encouraged, and (10) Other Important Educational Aspects.[204]

It seems important that competent evaluators of educational material have a broad educational background with expertness in one or more fields such as literature, history, or science. Such may be the case, but Mrs. Gabler describes her qualifications as a mother and housewife. Mr. Gabler is a retired Exxon clerk.[205] There is little doubt that the Gablers have influenced many parents in becoming arbiters of instructional materials.

An accusation brought against educators by well-organized political interests of the New and Evangelical far-right, particularly the pro-family coalition, is the claim that a "religion" called secular humanism is permeating the public schools.[206] The accusation is particularly confusing to many educators who do not understand the concept or context of the charge.

Two issues seem to be at the center of the charge: (1) the fact that public schools cannot teach religion, and (2) the humanistic philosophy of education which supports the

---

204. Educational Research Analysts, Inc., "Textbook Reviewing by Categories," Longview, Texas, n.d. (Mimeographed.)

205. Parker, "Your Schools May Be the Next Battlefield," p. 23.

206. J. Charles Park, "The New Right: Threat to Democracy in Education," *Educational Leadership* 38 (November, 1980): 146-49.

belief that education should be sensitive to the needs of students.[207] Humanistic philosophy has different interpretations to explicate its role within the field of education and needs clarification by educational leaders.[208]

Explaining and clarifying the term "secular humanism" as a "religion" is not an easy task. The Gablers' organization, Educational Research Analysts, defines secular humanism as a religion that "believes man is God and rejects biblical standards of living."[209] The Christophers, a religious group based in New York City, explains secular humanism as a trend that "places man at the center of the universe, designating him as the supreme ruler of Human destiny."[210]

The organizations, which claim that secular humanism is the "religion" of public schools, have apparently combined such dictionary definitions as:

> secular—of or pertaining to worldly things that are not regarded as religious, spiritual, or sacred; temporal . . . humanism—any system of thought or action based on the nature, dignity, interest, and ideals of man, specif., a modern, nontheistic, rationalist movement that holds that man is capable of self-fulfillment, ethical conduct, etc. without recourse to supernaturalism; the study of humanities . . .[211]

The gratuitous compounding of the two words seems to have given rise to a new label from which certain groups have created a bogus "religion" for public education.

Along with such definitions, the aforementioned groups

---

207. *Ibid.*, p. 148.

208. *Ibid.*, p. 149.

209. Educational Research Analysts, Inc., Longview, Texas, n.d. (Untitled Mimeographed Sheet.)

210. *Christopher Ideas,* The Christophers, 12 East 48th Street, New York, N.Y., n.d. (Printed Sheet.)

211. *Webster's New World Dictionary of the English Language,* 2d college ed. (New York: World Publishing Co., 1970).

cite a footnote in the Supreme Court's *Torcaso*[212] decision. The case concerned a man who was refused a commission in the Office of Notary Public of Maryland because he would not declare his belief in God. The Court with Justice Hugo Black writing the majority opinion ruled in favor of the plaintiff, saying in part:

> We repeat and again reaffirm that neither a State nor the Federal Government can constitutionally force a person "to profess a belief or disbelief in religion." Neither can constitutionally pass laws to impose requirements which aid all religions as against non-believers, and neither can aid those religions based on a belief in the existence of God as against those religions founded on different beliefs.[213]

The above quote plus footnote eleven referred to in the above paragraph is the legal basis given by religious groups who maintain that secular humanism is a religion. Footnote eleven states:

> Among religions in this country which do not teach what would generally be considered a belief in the existence of God are Buddhism, Taoism, Ethical Culture, Secular Humanism, and others.[214]

The same groups cite the *Seeger*[215] case which concerned conscientious objectors but which contains no mention of secular humanism. Thus, there appears to be no basis for a definition of secular humanism as presented by the New and Evangelical right.

Justice Hugo Black established a very narrow interpretation of the term *God* in the *Torcaso* decision. A broader

---

212. Torcaso v. Watkins, 367 U.S. 488, 81 S. Ct. 1680, 6 L. Ed. 2d 982 (1961).

213. *Ibid.*, p. 495.

214. *Ibid.*

215. United States v. Seeger, 380 U.S. 163, 85 S. Ct. 850, 13 L. Ed. 2d 733 (1965).

interpretation might include a universal being or spirit and an encapsulating world order. Certain Buddists and Taoists believe in God, and Ethical Culturalists believe in a world order which was the Supreme Court's position in *Seeger.* The assertion that public schools are teaching a Godless form of religion known as secular humanism is not logical and is full of redundancy. Professor Joseph E. Bryson has recognized the tautology:

> Based on the definition of religion if it is Godless then it cannot be a religion. However, linguistic analyses and logical deduction do not often play a major role when people are searching for reasons to justify an action. . . . The difficult question is, "What is Caesar's and what is God's?" or "What is secular not protected by the First Amendment freedom of religion?" In a democracy where politics and religion have a historical connection they are difficult to separate, but they are not inseparable in logic. As a point in example democracy is moral even to those who do not believe in God, and many believers in God do not believe in a democracy.[216]

Organizations further point to Humanist Manifesto I, issued in 1933 and signed by John Dewey and Humanist Manifesto II, issued in 1973 and signed by B.F. Skinner.[217] Since these two documents were signed by prominent educators, and since many educators follow the teachings of these two men, it follows, according to the accusers, that all public school educators embrace the philosophy of the two documents which the New and Evangelical right consider secular humanistic. Parenthetically, and while it may be a sad commentary on John Dewey's absolute influence, most

---

216. Joseph E. Bryson, *Current Church-State Issues,* address delivered to The Virginia School Law Conference. Virginia Polytechnic Institute, Blacksburg, Virginia, November, 1981. (Typewritten.)

217. Robert T. Rhode, "Is Secular Humanism the Religion of the Public Schools? " in *Dealing with Censorship,* ed. James E. Davis (Urbana: National Council of Teachers of English, 1979), pp. 122-23.

people who praise John Dewey have never read him and conversely most people who criticize John Dewey have never read him. It is doubtful that many school teachers have ever read John Dewey.

On this basis organizations such as the Heritage Foundation, Educational Research Analysts, Parents Watching the Schools, and the Moral Majority focus attacks on the public schools and their staffs.[218] The groups maintain that children no longer believe in God after exposure to secular humanism.[219] Sex education, values clarification, humanities courses, and science courses emphasizing Darwin's theory of evolution are particular targets for the groups.[220]

Behind the confusing controversy of secular humanism lies the basic premise of the purpose of the American public school. The New and Evangelical right appears to view the public school as a place of indoctrination to truth and values as viewed by the groups themselves, a place where access to information and ideas is to be suppressed or limited.[221] In order to educate children in a pluralistic, democratic society and prepare them for a diverse, changing world, it appears that educators will have to be aware of pressures which invite censorship and prevent opportunities for students to think, learn, and explore ideas.

§ 2.5. Summary.

A review of pertinent literature clearly points out that censorship is a real problem for public schools. Any level of public education may be confronted with controversy con-

---

218. *Ibid.*, pp. 117-19.
219. *Ibid.*, p. 121.
220. *Ibid.*, p. 118.
221. Park, "The New Right," p. 149.

cerning library books, textbooks, films, periodicals, instructional materials, or matters involving curriculum.

The censor may be a parent, an interested member of the community, a local or national organization, a teacher, a librarian, a student, a principal, the superintendent, or even the school board. Censorship attempts may or may not be reported in the news media. They may or may not be settled to the satisfaction of the complainant or the school. Solutions may involve litigation.

Controversy concerning schools is influenced by those problems generally encountered in society. Prevailing social, political, and religious trends influence community pressures on schools. Furthermore, censorship involves major legal issues such as academic freedom, students' rights, the rights of parents to direct their children's education, and the authority of school administrators and school boards.

In summation, censorship has been intertwined with mankind's destiny since earliest history. Seeds planted throughout history by philosophers such as Plato, Socrates, and Aristotle as well as various powerful political figures, were further nurtured by the work of Bowdler, Comstock, and Judge Cockburn. The result has been a profuse growth of censorship in society, including practically all media relating to education.

Those most concerned with publishing and education could well be participants in a continuing censorship "legacy" requiring court probate which may never be resolved to the satisfaction of all involved.

Chapter 3

THE LEGAL ASPECTS OF CENSORSHIP OF PUBLIC SCHOOL LIBRARY AND INSTRUCTIONAL MATERIALS

§ 3.0. Introduction.
§ 3.1. A Framework for Analyzing Legal Aspects of Censorship of Public School Library and Instructional Materials.
   A. Academic Freedom of Public School Teachers.
   B. Right of Students to Read and Receive Information.
   C. School Board Authority to Select and Remove Library and Instructional Materials.
   D. Parents' Right to Direct Education of Children.
   E. Religious Freedom of Public School Students, Related to Use of Library and Instructional Materials.
§ 3.2. Evolution of Legal Definition of Obscenity.
§ 3.3. Censorship Cases.
   A. Cases Supporting School Board Action.
   B. Cases Supporting Constitutional Rights.
§ 3.4. Summary.

§ 3.0. Introduction.

Controversy concerning public school curricular deci-sion-making and books and materials used for its imple-mentation is complex in nature, enmeshed in prevailing political and societal change. State legislatures and courts as well as federal courts and the United States Congress possess power and limitation over what is taught and how students are taught in public schools.

Decisions by the United States Supreme Court and lesser federal courts along with state courts have influenced curriculum, organization and administration of schools since 1879.[1] Many decisions relate directly or indirectly to

---

1. United States v. Bennett, 16 Blatch 338, Fed. Case 14, 571 (1879).

71

censorship of public school library and instructional materials.

Federal courts do not deal directly with educational concerns of public schools because the United States Constitution does not specifically mention education.[2] Moreover, federal jurists in rendering decisions have so often lamented that courts do not wish to become involved in day-to-day operations or administrative practices of public schools.[3] Since public schools are governed by school boards, courts rarely substitute judicial judgement for that of representatives chosen by the people.

There are, nevertheless, two principal issues through which federal courts obtain jurisdiction in litigation involving public education: (1) alleged violation of constitutionally protected right, privilege, or immunity of an individual; and (2) validity questions of state or federal statutes under the United States Constitution.[4]

These two major issues have led to judicial involvement in controversies concerning school censorship. Constitutional questions fall into five major categories: (1) academic freedom of teachers; (2) right of students to read and receive information; (3) right of school boards to make educational decisions; (4) right of parents to oversee the education of their children; and (5) religious freedom of individuals. Controversies concerning state and local legislation mainly involve issues such as the prohibition of

---

2. John C. Hogan, *The Schools, the Courts, and the Public Interest* (Lexington, Massachusetts: Lexington Books, 1974), p. 6.

3. Epperson v. Arkansas, 393 U.S. 97, 89 S. Ct. 266, 21 L. Ed. 2d 228 (1968); Lindros v. Governing Bd., 108 Cal. Rptr., 185, 9 Cal. 3d 524, 510 P.2d 361 (1972), *cert. denied,* 414 U.S. 1112 (1973); Mailloux v. Kiley, 323 F. Supp. 1387 (D. Mass), *aff'd,* 448 F.2d 1242 (1st Cir. 1971); and Presidents Council, Dist. 25 v. Community School Bd., No. 25457 F.2d 289 (2d Cir.), *cert. denied,* 409 U.S. 998 (1972).

4. Hogan, *The Schools,* p. 8.

teaching foreign language or Darwin's theory of evolution.[5] The Supreme Court's definition of obscenity and the process through which it has evolved is presented. This is done in order to provide the legal background on which is based the Court's decisions concerning "objectionable" books and materials.

§ 3.1. A Framework for Analyzing Legal Aspects of Censorship of Public School Library and Instructional Materials.

A. ACADEMIC FREEDOM OF PUBLIC SCHOOL TEACHERS.

Historically, judicial attitudes toward academic freedom tend to change with prevailing educational theory and philosophy.[6] Acceptance of academic freedom in American universities began in the late 1800s. The same acceptance of freedom to teach was never extended to elementary and secondary education.[7] The role of university education became generally accepted as one involving the pursuit of learning through scholarly teaching, research, publication, and service to the region, state, and nation. The traditional role of public schools, on the other hand, was viewed as one which was mainly concerned with indoctrination or transmission of community mores and established thought.[8]

In 1923 the Supreme Court made its initial ruling concerning the public school curriculum. Legislation in Nebraska prohibited the teaching of German to students below the eighth grade in public and non-public schools. The Supreme Court insisted that such legislation violated

---

5. Epperson v. Arkansas, 393 U. S. 97, 89 S. Ct. 266, 21 L. Ed. 2d 228 (1968).
6. "Academic Freedom in the Public Schools: The Right to Teach," *New York University Law Review* 48 (December, 1978): 1176-78.
7. *Ibid.*, p. 1179.
8. *Ibid.*

73

the liberty interest guaranteed by the Fourteenth Amendment.[9] Moreover, Justice McReynolds writing the majority opinion insisted that such legislation interfered with the rights of teachers to pursue their profession and with the rights of parents to educate and control their children.[10]

The last two decades brought about significant changes in public schools. With these changes emerged a group of educators who disavow the indoctrination theory. Currently many educational theorists support broad intellectual inquiry and the development of students' critical faculties as the function of elementary and secondary public schools rather than one of indoctrination.[11] Many such educators are proponents of "open" or "informal" education and view classrooms as a "marketplace of ideas." The central purpose of American education as stated by the Education Policies Commission is to produce "a rational thinking individual, who has developed both critical and creative thinking, and who uses these intellectual abilities in becoming a useful and productive member of society."[12] Recently this philosophy has achieved some acceptance as courts have

---

9. Meyer v. Nebraska, 262 U.S. 390, 43 S. Ct. 625, 67 L. Ed. 1042 (1923).

10. *Ibid.*

11. Roland S. Barth, *Open Education and the American School* (New York: Agathon Press, 1972); John Holt, *How Children Fail* (New York: Dell, 1965); Herbert R. Kohl, *The Open Classroom: A Practical Guide to a New Way of Teaching* (New York: Random House, 1969); Neill Postman and Charles Weingartner, *Teaching as a Subversive Activity* (New York: Dell, 1969).

12. Educational Policies Commission, *The Central Purpose of American Education* (Washington, D. C.: National Education Association, 1962), p. 12. See also Lawrence A. Cremin, *The Transformation of the School* (New York: Alfred A. Knopf, 1961).

begun to explore the right to teach. In *Sweezy*[13] Chief Justice Earl Warren noted:

> Scholarship cannot flourish in an atmosphere of suspicion and distrust. Teachers and students must always remain free to inquire, to study and to evaluate, to gain new maturity and understanding; otherwise, our civilization will stagnate and die.[14]

Although Justice Warren spoke primarily of college faculty and students, the observation is no less applicable at elementary and secondary levels of public education.[15]

The Supreme Court has recognized that "education is perhaps the most important function of state and local governments,"[16] and public school education is the primary vehicle which exposes children to the world around them and integrates them into society.[17] Since the *Brown I* decision the courts have begun to examine the role of education in a democratic society as well as the constitutional limits involved in the right to teach.

In *Keyishian*[18] the Supreme Court quoted *United States v. Associated Press*,[19] saying an education system best serves democracy when it teaches "through wide exposure to that robust exchange of ideas which discovers truth 'out of a multitude of tongues rather than through any kind of authoritative selection.' "[20] Justice William Brennan

---

13. Sweezy v. New Hampshire, 354 U.S. 234, 77 S. Ct. 1203, 1 L. Ed. 2d 1311 (1957).

14. *Ibid.*, 354 U.S., p. 250.

15. "Academic Freedom," *New York University Law Review,* p. 1183.

16. Brown v. Board of Educ., 347 U.S. 483, 493, 74 S. Ct. 686, 98 L. Ed. 873 (1954).

17. *Ibid.*

18. Keyishian v. Board of Regents, 385 U.S. 589, 87 S. Ct. 675, 17 L. Ed. 2d 629 (1967).

19. 326 U.S. 1, 65 S. Ct. 1416, 89 L. Ed. 1954 (1945).

20. Keyishian v. Board of Regents, supra note 18, p. 683.

writing the Court's majority opinion also expressed concern for the First Amendment freedom to create "a marketplace of ideas" in schools, thus supporting the creation of an intellectual atmosphere beneficial to teachers as well as for student inquiry.[21] An acceptance of the public school as a "marketplace of ideas" is not unanimous,[22] likewise, the absolute control of state over teaching has been challenged. In *Albaum*[23] the Federal District Court addresses the issue:

> The considerations which militate in favor of academic freedom—our historical commitment to free speech for all, the peculiar importance of academic inquiry to the progress of society, the need that both teacher and student operate in an atmosphere of open inquiry, feeling always free to challenge and improve established ideas—are relevant to elementary and secondary schools as well as to institutions of higher learning.[24]

The landmark *Tinker*[25] case, although dealing primarily with students' rights, has had a profound influence on the academic freedom of teachers. Justice Abe Fortas mentioned that:

> First Amendment rights, applied in light of the special characteristics of the school environment, are available to teachers and students. It can hardly be argued that either students or teachers shed their constitutional rights to freedom of speech or expression at the schoolhouse gate.[26]

---

21. *Ibid.,* pp. 683-84.

22. Sheldon H. Nahmod, "Controversy in the Classroom: The High School Teacher and Freedom of Expression," *George Washington Law Review* 39 (1971); 1032.

23. Albaum v. Carey, 283 F. Supp. 8 (E.D.N.Y. 1968).

24. *Ibid.,* p. 11.

25. Tinker v. Des Moines Indep. Community School Dist., 393 U.S. 503, 89 S. Ct. 733, 21 L. Ed. 2d 731 (1969).

26. *Ibid.,* p. 506.

The Court decision in *Tinker*[27] established a precedent which has been followed in case law since 1969.

It seems clear that the classroom teacher's right to exercise professional responsibility in teaching is presently a judicially cognizable right and is constitutionally based on the First Amendment.[28] A unified legal definition of academic rights for public school teachers has still not emerged. Therefore, the scope of protection available has relied on contracts and due process. All fifty states have a compelling interest in the education and welfare of children and this is always a major consideration. Currently the trend of courts is to develop a balance between state autonomy of public education and the right to teach.[29]

B. RIGHT OF STUDENTS TO READ AND RECEIVE INFORMATION.

Rapid societal change has brought with it expanded rights to minors. The extension of constitutional rights to young people has not been an organized movement. Instead it has resulted chiefly from litigation concerning prohibition of specific student activities by public school officials.[30] Although passage of the Twenty-sixth Amendment,[31]

---

27. *Ibid.*

28. Meyer v. Nebraska, 262 U.S. 390 (1923), pp. 400-01; Sweezy v. New Hampshire, 354 U.S. 234, 77 S. Ct. 1203, 1 L. Ed. 2d 1311 (1957), pp. 248-50; Keyishian v. Board of Regents, 385 U.S. 589, 87 S. Ct. 675, 17 L. Ed. 2d 629 (1967), p. 603; Tinker v. Des Moines Indep. Community School Dist., 393 U.S. 503, 89 S. Ct. 733, 21 L. Ed. 2d 731 (1969), p. 506; Parducci v. Rutland, 316 F. Supp. 352 (M.D. Ala. 1970), pp. 354-55; Mailloux v. Kiley, 323 F. Supp. 1387 (D. Mass.), *aff'd,* 448 F.2d 1242 (1st Cir. 1971); Moore v. Gaston County Bd. of Educ., 357 F. Supp. 1037 (W.D.N.C. 1973); and Lindros v. Governing Bd., 108 Cal. Rptr. 185, 9 Cal. 3d 524, 510 P. 2d 361, *cert. denied,* 414 U.S. 1112 (1973).

29. "Academic Freedom," *New York University Law Review,* p. 1190.

30. Richard Gyory, "The Constitutional Rights of Public School Pupils," *Fordham Law Review* 40 (1971): 201.

31. U.S. Const. amend. XXVI.

which extended the right to vote to eighteen year-old citizens, was influential in generally expanding rights, the major thrust has been through case law.[32] The primary gain in students' rights before 1969 was on the college and university level.[33] Since that time a major focus has been on the rights of high school students.[34]

Two major Supreme Court decisions expanded the constitutional rights of students. First in 1967 the Supreme Court encapsulated procedural due process for students of all ages.[35] Second, the 1975 *Goss*[36] decision insisted that students be given a due process hearing before suspension and/or dismissal. Moreover, in the 1975 *Wood*[37] decision the Court maintained that when students' constitutional rights are violated school board members could be held liable under the Civil Rights Act of 1871.

In the 1969 *Tinker*[38] case the Supreme Court made its first unambiguous assertion concerning First Amendment rights of school children. Justice Fortas maintained that:

> It can hardly be argued that either students or teachers shed their constitutional rights to freedom of speech or expression at the schoolhouse gate.[39]

---

32. Brown v. Board of Educ., 347 U.S. 483, 74 S. Ct. 686, 98 L. Ed. 873 (1954); Kent v. United States, 383 U.S. 541, 86 S. Ct. 1045, 16 L. Ed. 2d 84 (1966); In re Gault, 387 U.S. 1, 87 S. Ct. 1428, 18 L. Ed. 2d 527 (1967); Tinker v. Des Moines Indep. Community School Dist., 393 U.S. 503, 89 S. Ct. 733, 21 L. Ed. 2d 731 (1969).

33. Tinker v. Des Moines, *supra* note 32.

34. Gyory, "Constitutional Rights," *Fordham Law Review,* p. 201.

35. In re Gault, 387 U.S. 1, 87 S. Ct. 1428, 18 L. Ed. 2d 527 (1967).

36. Goss v. Lopez, 419 U.S. 565, 95 S. Ct. 729, 42 L. Ed. 2d 725 (1975).

37. Wood v. Strickland, 420 U.S. 308, 95 S. Ct. 992, 43 L. Ed. 2d 214 (1974).

38. Tinker v. Des Moines, *supra* note 32.

39. *Ibid.,* p. 506.

Tinker was significant in extending judicial concern to areas formerly omitted from legal process.[40] Even in *Tinker* caution was expressed by Justice Potter Stewart's concurring opinion which stated in part that a child does not possess the "full capacity for individual choice which is the presupposition of First Amendment guarantees." [41] Nevertheless, as a result of the *Tinker* decision, it is now customary for federal courts to review the constitutional rights of public school students when petitioned to do so.

Justice Oliver Wendell Holmes identified the library as "a marketplace of ideas" as early as 1919.[42] In spite of Justice Holmes' enlightened concept, the censorship of library materials has become increasingly important as a legal issue involving public school students' right to read, to know, to learn, and to be informed. States entrust school boards with the privilege of selecting books and materials. When this results in alleged violations of legislative and constitutional considerations, controversy results.

As early as 1879, a federal court in New York addressed the question of students' right to receive information.[43] During the intervening years, the federal courts have addressed this issue on many occasions. And in recent years, courts have sometimes insisted that school board conservatism encroaches on students' rights. Since 1973, complaints of obscenity under the *Miller* [44] test alone have rendered few materials inaccessible to students.

These recent Supreme Court decisions support the constitutional right to receive information. Although none

---

40. Gyory, "Constitutional Rights," *Fordham Law Review,* p. 214.

41. Tinker v. Des Moines, *supra* note 32, p. 515.

42. Abrams v. United States, 250 U.S. 616, 630, 40 S. Ct. 17, 63 L. Ed. 1173 (1919).

43. United States v. Bennett, 16 Blatch 338, Fed. Case 14, 571 (1879).

44. Miller v. California, 413 U.S. 15, 93 S. Ct. 2607, 37 L. Ed. 2d 419 (1973).

of these cases refers specifically to minors, both students and federal jurists have cited these cases in subsequent school censorship cases. The 1972 *Kleindienst*[45] decision confirmed First Amendment right to receive information. In *Virginia State Board of Pharmacy*[46] the Court, relying, on *Kleindienst*[47] maintained: "We acknowledge that this court has referred to a First Amendment right to 'receive information and ideas,' and that freedom of speech 'necessarily protects the rights to receive.' "[48]

In 1978, *Pacifica*[49] introduced a new dimension into censorship of school library and instruction materials even though the case concerned the spoken rather than written word.[50] The five to four Supreme Court decision allowed the Federal Communication Commission to regulate "indecent" as well as obscene broadcast during hours when children are most likely to listen.[51] In the most recent censorship 1982 *Pico*[52] decision, the Supreme Court, with Justice

---

45. Kleindienst v. Mandel, 408 U.S. 753, 92 S. Ct. 2576, 33 L. Ed. 2d 683 (1972), pp. 762-763.

46. Virginia State Bd. of Pharmacy v. Virginia Citizens' Consumer Council, Inc., 425 U.S. 748, 96 S. Ct. 1817, 48 L. Ed. 2d 346 (1976).

47. Kleindienst v. Mandel, *supra* note 45.

48. Virginia State Bd. of Pharmacy, *supra* note 46, p. 757.

49. Federal Communications Comm'n v. Pacifica Found., 438 U.S. 726, 98 S. Ct. 3026, 57 L. Ed. 2d 1073 (1978).

50. M. Chester Nolte, "New Pig in the Parlor: Official Constraints on Indecent Words," *NOLPE School Law Journal* 9 (1980): 2.

51. Federal Communications Comm'n v. Pacifica Found., *supra* note 49, pp. 3040-41.

52. Board of Educ. v. Pico, Case No. 80-2043, 50 L.W. 4831 (1982); See also Pratt v. Independent School Dist. No. 831, 670 F.2d 771 (8th Cir. 1982). Here the Eighth Circuit Court of Appeals insisted that a school board policy, removing two films "The Lottery" and a "trailer film," that was predicated on political and religious ideological views, violated students' First Amendment free speech by denying them the right to receive information; See also Martin v. City of Struthers, 318 U.S. 141,

William Brennan writing the opinion insisted that school children had the right to receive information and ideas. Such right is predicated on First Amendment free speech and press and encapsulates a First Amendment right for the "sender" to disseminate information and the "receiver" right to receive ideas and information.

Case law confirms that rights of minors have increased, particularly since the 1969 *Tinker*[53] decision. The right to read and receive information by public school students has not been conclusively settled by the courts. Future case law concerning the right of public school students to read, to know, and to be informed will probably be dealt with in case-by-case consideration rather than by following an established pattern.[54]

C. SCHOOL BOARD AUTHORITY TO SELECT AND REMOVE LIBRARY AND INSTRUCTIONAL MATERIALS.

School boards are empowered through state statutes to prescribe curricula. Authority to select textbooks, library books, and other instructional materials is derived from the same source.[55] It logically follows that school personnel, librarians and teachers, do not have unreviewable privileges to select library and instructional materials. Within the scope of school boards is authority to approve or disapprove such action.[56] However, there are constitutional

---

143, 63 S. Ct. 862, 87 L. Ed. 1313 (1943) and Lamont v. Postmaster General, 381 U.S. 301, 308 (1965) for a more detailed treatment of the First Amendment "sender-receiver" concept.

53. Tinker v. Des Moines Indep. Community School Dist., 393 U.S. 503, 89 S. Ct. 733, 21 L. Ed. 2d 731 (1969).

54. Gyory, "Constitutional Rights," *Fordham Law Review*, p. 224.

55. Bolmeier, *School in the Legal Structure*, p. 100.

56. Julia Turnquist Bradley, "Censoring the School Library: Do Students Have the Right to Read?" *Connecticut Law Review* 10 (Spring, 1978): 757.

limitations on the discretion of school boards to review and remove books and materials from school libraries.

The Supreme Court has described the First Amendment as having "preferred position" over other considerations.[57] The Court also stated:

> If there is any fixed star in our constitutional constellation, it is that no official, high or petty, can prescribe what shall be orthodox in politics, nationalism, religion, or other matters of opinion.[58]

Matters of taste and style are included in First Amendment protection,[59] and obscenity at this point is still not an issue for judicial consideration.[60] Courts have protected school boards when "unduly sensitive persons" objected to books or materials.[61]

On occasion school boards have attempted to justify their own censorship actions through statutory discretion over book selections.[62] Sometimes school boards have acted with indifference toward constitutional concerns.[63]

---

57. Kovacs v. Cooper, 336 U.S. 77, 88, 69 S. Ct. 448, 93 L. Ed. 513 (1949).

58. West Virginia State Bd. of Educ. v. Barnette, 319 U.S. 624, 63 S. Ct. 1178, 87 L. Ed. 1628 (1943), p. 42.

59. Hannegan v. Esquire, Inc., 327 U.S. 146, 157-58, 66 S. Ct. 456, 90 L. Ed. 586 (1946).

60. Roth v. United States, 354 U.S. 476, 77 S. Ct. 1304, 1 L. Ed. 2d 1498 (1957); Miller v. California, 431 U.S. 115, 93 S. Ct. 2607, 37 L. Ed. 2d 419 (1973).

61. Rosenberg v. Board of Educ., 196 Misc. 542, 92 N.Y.S.2d 344, 346 (Sup. Ct. 1949).

62. Pico v. Board of Educ., 474 F. Supp. 387 (E.D.N.Y. 1979), rev'd and remanded, 638 F.2d 404 (2d Cir. 1980); Board of Educ. v. Pico, Case No. 80-2043, 50 L.W. 4831 (1982).

63. Keefe v. Geanakos, 305 F. Supp. 1091 (D. Mass.), reversed and remanded, 418 F.2d 359 (1st Cir. 1969).

The Court's *Tinker*[64] decision has greatly affected the litigious posture of school boards. Expanded constitutional rights of students have "largely taken place as the results of conflict with school administrators."[65] Since the landmark *Tinker* decision in 1969, school boards and school districts usually appear in court as defendants. Plaintiffs are generally pupils, teachers, parents, and taxpayers. Although *Tinker* did not deal directly with procedural due process, schools have been forced to view that area more closely than in the past.

Another effect of *Tinker* is that school boards have had to shoulder the burden of proof, justifying actions and regulations. The testimony of school officials has less relative weight than before 1969.[66] Judgmental statements by expert educators are not as easily accepted by courts as they were in the past. In other words, the trend has moved away from unquestioning acceptance of testimony by school authorities.

If courts view the traditional role of public schools as being centers of indoctrination and transmission of community mores, then schools have almost unlimited power to select and review library books and instructional materials.[67] On the other hand, if courts view the public school as a marketplace of ideas, the constitutional rights of students and teachers must then be given full consideration.[68]

---

64. Tinker v. Des Moines Indep. Community School Dist., 393 U.S. 503, 89 S. Ct. 733, 21 L. Ed. 2d 731 (1969).

65. Gyory, *Fordham Law Review*, p. 237.

66. *Ibid.*, p. 235.

67. Mailloux v. Kiley, 323 F. Supp. 1387, 1392 (D. Mass.), *aff'd*, 448 F.2d 1242 (1st Cir. 1971).

68. Minarchini v. Strongsville City School Dist., 384 F. Supp. 698 (N.D. Ohio 1974), *aff'd in part, rev'd in part*, 541 F.2d 577 (6th Cir. 1976).

Restriction of sources such as library books by school boards has been considered a serious constitutional concern.[69] Although students might obtain the same materials from another source, the Supreme Court has asserted that exercise of constitutional rights could not be abridged at certain times and places merely because they could be exercised at other times and places.[70]

A school library differs from a classroom in that students are not required to read particular books but may choose at will what is to be read. Libraries present a wide variety of materials and do not advocate or oppose philosophies presented by books or materials.[71]

Selection and censorship are distinguishable. Selection is a process whereby specific materials are chosen from all available materials, limited only by educational considerations, budget, and space. Censorship, on the other hand, permanently limits access to books and materials based on the value or prejudice of an individual or group.[72] An article in the *Connecticut Law Review* states:

> [A] case in which a school board seeks to censor library books provides the court with an ideal opportunity to apply principles of academic freedom to secondary schools, without judicially mandating a particular theory of educational purpose and without altering the traditional structure of American education.[73]

Recent decisions illustrate that courts have divided opinions on school board censorship. Although courts generally

---

69. Schneider v. State, 308 U.S. 147, 60 S. Ct. 146, 84 L. Ed. 155 (1939).

70. Spence v. Washington, 418 U.S. 405, 411, 94 S. Ct. 2727, 41 L. Ed. 2d 842 (1974).

71. "Comment: School Boards, Schoolbooks, and the Freedom to Learn," *Yale Law Review* 59 (1950): 953-54.

72. Bradley, "Censoring the School Library," *Connecticut Law Review,* p. 770.

73. *Ibid.*

uphold school boards in day-to-day administration of schools, recent case law establishes a trend toward upholding both academic freedom of teachers and students' right to receive information.

D. PARENTS' RIGHT TO DIRECT EDUCATION OF CHILDREN.

In the late 1800s, parents' rights to direct the education of their children was unquestionable. The state obligation was to provide tax-supported schools to which parents might entrust their children's education.[74]

In a 1923 decision,[75] the right of the child to receive an education did not stand alone. The Supreme Court insisted the prohibition by Nebraska law to teach German to students below eighth grade was "an arbitrary interference with the liberty of parents to control and educate their children." [76] Two years later in *Pierce*,[77] a case concerning compulsory public school attendance in Oregon, the Court maintained that such legislation "unreasonably interferes with the liberty of parents and guardians to direct the upbringing and education of children under their control."[78]

It was not until 1954 that focus began to change from parents' rights to the rights and welfare of children.[79] Probably no other Supreme Court decision has had a greater influence on American society than that in *Brown*

---

74. Joel S. Moskowitz, "Parental Rights and State Education," *Washington Law Review* 50 (1975): 623.

75. Meyer v. Nebraska, 262 U.S. 390, 43 S. Ct. 625, 67 L. Ed. 1042 (1923).

76. Bolmeier, *School in the Legal Structure,* p. 10.

77. Pierce v. Society of Sisters of the Holy Names of Jesus and Mary, 268 U.S. 510, 534-35, 45 S. Ct. 571, 69 L. Ed. 1070 (1925).

78. *Ibid.*

79. Gyory, "Constitutional Rights," *Fordham Law Review,* p. 203.

I.[80] Although the drama involved in the case emphasized equal education, it was a child-oriented decision. Richard Gyory wrote in the *Fordham Law Review:*

> Prior to 1954, the context in which the Court dealt with educational matters was either the claims of adults to equal access to higher education or actions which mingled the rights of parents and taxpayers.[81]

The full impact of students' constitutional rights was not fully realized until *Tinker*[82] in 1969.

The Supreme Court's *Yoder*[83] decision is a most significant case involving parents' rights and public education. Amish parents claimed the compulsory attendance law of Wisconsin violated First and Fourteenth Amendment rights. School attendance after age sixteen was contrary to Amish religious belief and way of life. This case weighed the right of parents to oversee the education of their children versus state control. "Thus, the *Yoder* Court held that the parents' common law right to direct their children's education, combined with the constitutional guarantee of freedom of religion, displaces the compulsory attendance statute."[84] In a dissenting opinion, Justice William O. Douglas insisted that the child should express his desire on the subject rather than having the parents' views imposed on him.[85] It is intuitively obvious that the Supreme Court in *Yoder* has ele-

---

80. Brown v. Board of Educ., 347 U.S. 483, 74 S. Ct. 686, 98 L. Ed. 873 (1954).

81. Gyory, "Constitutional Rights," *Fordham Law Review,* p. 203.

82. Tinker v. Des Moines Indep. Community School Dist., 393 U.S. 503, 89 S. Ct. 733, 21 L. Ed. 2d 731 (1969).

83. Wisconsin v. Yoder, 406 U. S. 205, 92 S. Ct. 1526, 32 L. Ed. 2d 15 (1972).

84. Joel S. Moskowitz, "Parental Rights and State Education," *Washington Law Review* 50 (1975): 629.

85. Wisconsin v. Yoder, supra note 83, pp. 241-43.

vated the First Amendment religious freedom above the other First Amendment freedoms.

Another case which has applied the balancing test requiring schools to follow parents' requests is *Glaser*.[86] A parent forbade school authorities to use corporal punishment on a child. The court ruled the school must defer to the wishes of the parent unless the decision "will jeopardize the health or safety of the child, or have a potential for significant social burdens."[87]

In spite of the *Yoder* and *Glaser* decisions, the trend of courts at present seems to be toward emphasis of students' rights rather than parents' rights. After examining the legal background, it is not surprising that public school censorship cases in the last two decades have placed more emphasis on rights of students to read, to learn, and to receive information than on the rights of parents to direct education of children. "The minor may still have to share his legal billing in the captioned credits with his parents, but there is no longer any question as to who is the star." [88]

E. RELIGIOUS FREEDOM OF PUBLIC SCHOOL STUDENTS, RELATED TO USE OF LIBRARY AND INSTRUCTIONAL MATERIALS.

The establishment clause of the First Amendment [89] is the basis for substantive restriction on what can be taught in public schools. "Congress shall make no law respecting an establishment of religion"[90] is equally applicable to states through the Fourteenth Amendment.[91]

---

86. Glaser v. Marietta, 351 F. Supp. 555 (W.D. Pa. 1972).

87. *Ibid.*, p. 559.

88. Gyory, "Constitutional Rights," *Fordham Law Review,* p. 206.

89. U.S. Const. amend. I.

90. *Ibid.*

91. U.S. Const. amend. XIV.

Few Supreme Court cases based on the establishment clause have dealt directly with actual instructional practices or uses of books and materials in public schools. In 1948 the Supreme Court in *McCollum*[92] insisted that on campus religious studies programs for instruction in individual faiths violated the First Amendment freedom of religion. Even though churches paid the salaries of teachers, tax-supported public buildings could not be used to promulgate religious doctrines to students.[93]

The Supreme Court *Epperson*[94] decision is among the most important cases in this area. Based on the Tennessee statute which was upheld in the famous *Scopes*[95] "monkey trial," Arkansas passed legislation providing criminal penalties and dismissal for any teacher presenting Darwin's theory of evolution in classrooms. Justice Abe Fortas writing the Court's opinion reaffirmed states' right to prescribe curriculum for public schools. A curriculum could clearly include teaching Bible as history or literature, but in the process of teaching, schools must remain neutral in religious matters. However, Justice Fortas insisted that Arkansas' statute clearly violated First Amendment rights.[96] The statute was deemed to be in conflict since it tended to take sides with "a particular religious doctrine; that is, with a particular interpretation of the Book of Genesis by a particular religious group."[97]

---

92 McCollum v. Board of Educ., 333 U.S. 203, 68 S. Ct. 461, 92 L. Ed. 649 (1948).

93. *Ibid.*, pp. 463-65.

94. Epperson v. Arkansas, 393 U.S. 97, 89 S. Ct. 266, 21 L. Ed. 2d 228 (1968).

95. Scopes v. State, 154 Tenn. 105, 289 S.W. 363 (1927).

96. Epperson v. Arkansas, supra note 94, p. 103.

97. *Ibid.* In 1981 the Arkansas General Assembly once again signed into law a Genesis statute—the "balanced treatment statute"—and this statute was declared unconstitutional as First Amendment advancement

The constitutional question of Bible reading in public schools was the issue in *Schempp*.[98] The Pennsylvania statute required reading of at least ten Bible verses at opening of each school day without comment by teacher in charge. After a federal district court declared the statute unconstitutional, another sentence was added indicating that children could be excused upon written request from parents.

On appeal the United States Supreme Court declared the statute unconstitutional as First Amendment establishment of religion. Justice Tom Clark maintained that the statute preferred Christian religion since it required reading the Holy Bible. The primary intention of the statute was to introduce a religious ceremony into public schools. In his concurring opinion Justice William J. Brennan, Jr. indicated:

> What the Framers meant to foreclose, and what our decision under the Establishment Clause have forbidden, are those involvements of religious with secular institutions which (a) serve the essentially religious activities of religious institutions; (b) employ the organs of government for essentially religious means to serve governmental ends, where secular means would suffice.[99]

Justice Clark further pointed out "objective instruction in comparative religion or the history of religion and its relationship to the advancement of civilization" is important and proper for an educated citizenry.[100] The decision

---

of religion in McLean v. Arkansas Bd. of Educ., 529 F. Supp. 1255 (E.D. Ark. 1982).

98. School Dist. of Abington Township v. Schempp, 374 U.S. 203, 83 S. Ct. 1560, 10 L. Ed. 2d 844 (1963).

99. *Ibid.*, pp. 294-95.

100. *Ibid.*, p. 225.

was also applied to *Murray v. Curlett* [101] and later to *Chamberlain v. Dade County Board of Public Instruction.* [102] The obligatory nature of these ceremonies always influence the decisions.

Books discussing religion and sex often promote or suppress some religious belief. However, if use is based on sound educational purpose and does not support or suppress religious views, no establishment clause violation is created. [103] Some library books and instructional materials, nevertheless, may offend religious beliefs of parents or students. Compulsory use of these materials may create constitutional issues, particularly where students cannot be excused when conflict exists with values and religion.

In *West Virginia State Board of Education v. Barnette,* [104] the Court held that Jehovah's Witnesses could not be compelled to salute the United States flag in school. The 1973 Supreme Court *Yoder* [105] decision maintained that Amish children could not be compelled to attend school past eighth grade because of parents' religious beliefs. In both instances fundamental religious beliefs outweighed state's compelling interest in education. Where there is a religious concern then it should be intuitively obvious that if school boards require students to use certain library and instructional materials without providing an alternative assignment or excuse policy, free exercise of religion may be impaired. The judicial balancing process may involve the

---

101. 228 Md. 239, 179 A.2d 698 (1962).

102. 377 U.S. 402, 84 S. Ct. 1272, 12 L. Ed. 2d 407 (1964). See also Meitzer v. Board of Pub. Instruction of Orange City, 548 F.2d 559 (5th Cir. 1977).

103. Frederick F. Schauer, "School Books, Lesson Plans, and the Constitution," *West Virginia Law Review* 78 (May, 1976): 308-09.

104. 319 U.S. 624, 63 S. Ct. 1178, 87 L. Ed. 1628 (1943).

105. Wisconsin v. Yoder, 406 U.S. 205, 92 S. Ct. 1526, 32 L. Ed. 2d 15 (1972).

importance of books and materials. Different considerations may compel different decisions.[106]

Compulsory sex education in New Jersey [107] was ruled to encroach on parents' right to mold children's behavior in family and religious beliefs. In New York City a group of parents requested Charles Dickens' *Oliver Twist* and William Shakespeare's *Merchant of Venice* be removed from school libraries.[108] The books, according to plaintiffs, presented a stereotype of Jews which was offensive to members of that religious sect. However, the New York Supreme Court supported the school board and the books were retained. Another case [109] was based on a complaint that Kurt Vonnegut, Jr.'s *Slaughterhouse-Five* made reference to religious matters and contained obscenity. The Michigan Court of Appeals ruled for the school board on grounds that the book was intended to teach about religion rather than to indoctrinate a religious philosophy.

Parents in Kanawha County, West Virginia, protested textbooks and supplementary instructional materials which, among other assertions, they claimed ridiculed religious beliefs and groups.[110] In this case, too, the federal district court maintained that schools could teach about religion.

The area of sex education and books and films used in such courses sometimes become religious issues. In *Medeiros*[111] the parents of elementary students challenged

---

106. Schauer, "School Books," *West Virginia Law Review,* p. 313.

107. Valent v. New Jersey State Bd. of Educ., 114 N.J. Super. 63, 274 A.2d 832 (1971).

108. Rosenberg v. Board of Educ., 196 Misc. 542, 92 N.Y.S.2d 344 (Sup. Ct. 1949).

109. Todd v. Rochester Community Schools, 41 Mich. App. 320, 200 N.W.2d 90 (1972).

110. Williams v. Board of Educ., 388 F. Supp. 93 (S.D.W.V. 1975).

111. Madeiros v. Kiyosaki, 478 P.2d 314 (Hawaii 1970).

the showing of particular films as part of a sex education course on the basis that it was an invasion of privacy and violated religious freedom. Participation was not compulsory. Plaintiffs questioned whether or not "parents are free to educate their off-spring in the intimacies of sexual matters according to their own moral and religious beliefs without due interference from the state." [112] The Hawaii Supreme Court with Chief Justice Richardson writing the opinion, found for the school board. Justice Richardson maintained that:

> Inasmuch as we have found no compulsion or coercion related to the educational program in question we find no violation of the First Amendment's Free Exercise of Religion Clause.[113]

Emerging from case law is a three-fold test providing that: (1) state educational activity have a strictly secular purpose; (2) public education neither promotes nor inhibits religion; and (3) there be no governmental entanglement with religion.[114]

§ 3.2. Evolution of Legal Definition of Obscenity.

The obscenity issue, usually one or more passages, sits at midcenter of the majority of censorship debates. Since 1868 the United States Supreme Court has devoted myriads of hours and written thousands of words in an effort to define obscenity.

The judicial philosophy evolved through several stages.

------

112. *Ibid.,* p. 315.

113. *Ibid.,* p. 319.

114. Schauer, "School Books," *West Virginia Law Review* 78 (May, 1976): 308-09. For complete development of the Supreme Court's Tripart religious test see Lemon v. Kurtzman, 403 U.S. 602, 91 S. Ct. 2105 (1971). See also Walz v. Tax Comm'n, 397 U.S. 664, 90 S. Ct. 1409, 25 L. Ed. 2d 697 (1970).

Beginning with the *Hicklin* Doctrine in 1868, judicial decisions insisted that material harmful to children and to particularly susceptible individuals was harmful to everyone. Materials were judged obscene even though passages were often taken out of context or there was a single word or phrase that might be offensive.

The next obscenity definition phase distinguished between materials harmful to children but acceptable to adults. Finally, the Supreme Court established a test emphasizing the effect of material on the average person, application of contemporary standards, and consideration of the work as a whole to include literary and artistic merit. The following judicial decisions highlight some important and interesting ramifications of obscenity. Their effect on the selection and use of library books and instructional materials in public schools directly or indirectly influence the education of young people in a profound way.

The legal question of censorship pertaining to the use of books and materials by minors has been an issue since the *Hicklin* [115] decision in 1868. This case was the first legal effort to define a test for obscenity. The English Court ruled that intent of the author or publisher was not at issue in the case. Instead, the issue was "whether the tendency of the matter charged as obscenity is to deprave and corrupt those whose minds are open to such immoral influences, and into whose hands a publication of this sort might fall." [116] Thus, focus was placed on "particularly susceptible individuals" such as children rather than on the public at large. The *Hicklin* Test was considered a justification for obscenity laws. It was welcomed by courts in the United States.

In the 1913 *Kennerly* [117] case Judge Learned Hand

---

115. Regina v. Hicklin, 3 L.R.-Q.B. 360 (1868).
116. *Ibid.*, p. 371.
117. United States v. Kennerley, 209 F. 119 (S.D.N.Y. 1913).

handed down a decision concerning a novel about big city vice. Judge Hand acknowledged that his decision was anchored in the *Hicklin* logic. After all, suggested Justice Hand, the *Hicklin* logic had been used as precedent in lower courts, therefore he could not disregard it. However, Justice Hand added a statement to his decision which might have signaled a redirection of judicial philosophy:

> I hope it is not improper for me to say that the rule as laid down, however, consonant it may be with mid-Victorian morals, does not seem to me to answer to the understanding and morality of the present time, as conveyed by the words, "obscene, lewd, or lasciv-ious."[118]

The ruling in *Hicklin*[119] tended to limit reading matter for all adults to that suitable for children and the entire population. Justice Hand's statement, a departure from the *Hicklin* logic, manifested its influence in case law in a notable decision in 1933.

The decision in *One Book Called "Ulysses"*[120] rejected *Hicklin* without citing any authority. The court insisted that intent of an author toward pornography, i.e. exploitation of obscenity, must be determined before the work could be declared obscene. This decision considered the concept of an "average person." A book should be examined basically from the point of view of its literary value. It should be evaluated as a whole rather than through excerpts or mere words or phrases taken out of context. The new obscenity test was not universally accepted by all judges.

---

118. *Ibid.*, p. 121.

119. Regina v. Hicklin, supra note 115.

120. United States v. One Book Called "Ulysses," 5 F. Supp. 182 (S.D.N.Y. 1933), *aff'd,* 72 F.2d 705 (2d Cir. 1934).

In a 1945 case involving Lillian Smith's *Strange Fruit*,[121] the court asserted:

> [W]e are of the opinion that an honest and reasonable judge or jury could find beyond a reasonable doubt that this book "manifestly tends to corrupt the morals of youth." [122]

This decision rejected the excerpt approach and judged the book as a whole; however, literary merit of the work was not considered.

In the 1948 *Winters* [123] case, the Supreme Court recognized for the first time that substantial First Amendment rights are involved in laws which declared that distribution of "harmful" materials is criminal. The Court also recognized that even objectionable materials may be protected by the First Amendment. During the same year in *Doubleday*,[124] the Court fully discussed First Amendment rights related to obscenity laws. Since no opinion on the subject was rendered, the full impact of the discussion apparently did not carry great influence on future decisions.

In 1949 Judge Curtis Bok ruled on the obscenity of several modern novels.[125] Obscenity was not "mere coarseness or vulgarity" insisted Justice Bok. He also considered the restriction of freedom of speech through obscenity laws. Such laws should apply to the "sexually impure and pornographic." Even then there must be clear evidence that a

---

121. Commonwealth v. Isenstadt, 318 Mass. 543, 62 N.E.2d 840 (1945).

122. *Ibid.*, p. 840.

123. Winters v. New York, 333 U.S. 507, 68 S. Ct. 665, 92 L. Ed. 840 (1948).

124. Doubleday & Co. v. New York, 335 U.S. 848 (1948).

125. Commonwealth v. Feigenbaum, 166 Pa. Super. 120, 70 A.2d 389 (1950).

crime had been or was about to be committed as a result of the publication.[126]

Four years later in *Besig* [127] the Ninth Circuit Appeals Court tackled the obscenity issue in Henry Miller's *Tropic of Cancer* and *Tropic of Capricorn*. The court, in applying the "average person" test, wrote: "Dirty word description of the sweet and sublime, especially of the mystery of sex and procreation, is the ultimate of obscenity." [128]

In 1957 Justice Felix Frankfurter in the *Butler* [129] decision said adults should not be prohibited from reading certain materials just because the books and materials potentially may have a harmful effect on youth.

> The state insists that, by thus quarantining the general reading public against books not too rugged for grown men and women in order to shield juvenile innocence, it is exercising its power to promote the general welfare. Surely, this is to burn the house to roast the pig . . . We have before us legislation not unreasonably restricted to the evil with which it is said to deal. The incidence of this enactment is to reduce the adult population of Michigan to reading only what is fit for children.[130]

The United States Supreme Court modernized the definition and test for obscenity in the 1957 *Roth* [131] decision "whether to the average person, applying contemporary community standards, the dominant theme of the material taken as a whole appeals to the prurient interest." [132] This

---

126. Frederick F. Schauer, *The Law of Obscenity* (Washington: Bureau of National Affairs, 1976), p. 32.

127. Besig v. United States, 208 F.2d 142 (9th Cir. 1953).

128. *Ibid.*, p. 146.

129. Butler v. Michigan, 352 U.S. 380, 77 S. Ct. 524, 1 L. Ed. 2d 412 (1957).

130. *Ibid.*, p. 383.

131. Roth v. United States, 354 U.S. 476, 77 S.Ct. 1304, 1 L. Ed. 2d 1498 (1957).

132. *Ibid.*, p. 489.

was the first use of the term "contemporary community standards" by the Supreme Court. This concept was not new. It had been used in many lower court opinions such as *Kennerley* [133] and *Isenstadt*. [134]

The *Roth* [135] test moved toward an external standard for obscenity rather than accepting personal views and opinions regarding what should be proscribed. This decision also moved away from judging materials on the basis of their effect on "particularly susceptible individuals." Although the Court did not define the term "community," the lower court had instructed the jury to judge material by its influence upon the "average person in the community ... by present day standards." [136] The Supreme Court approved the lower court's instructions, and Chief Justice Earl Warren's concurring opinion supported the view. After *Roth* several lower courts adopted a local view toward "contemporary community standards."

In delivering the opinion in *Roth*,[137] Justice William J. Brennan, Jr. made a statement that later became highly controversial — "But implicit in the history of the First Amendment is the rejection of obscenity as utterly without redeeming social importance." [138]

As long as the *Hicklin* [139] test was acceptable to the Supreme Court, rulings on obscenity were fairly simple. If obscene material was harmful to minors, it should not be available to anyone. As the Supreme Court philosophy developed and only hard-core pornography was prohibited,

---

133. United States v. Kennerley, 209 F. 119 (S.D.N.Y. 1913).

134. Commonwealth v. Isenstadt, 318 Mass. 543, 62 N.E.2d 840 (1945).

135. Roth v. United States, supra note 131.

136. *Ibid.*, p. 490.

137. *Ibid.*

138. *Ibid.*, p. 492.

139. Regina v. Hicklin, 3 L.R.-Q.B. 360 (1868).

the question of obscene materials concerning minors gained importance.

The Supreme Court continued to be influenced by *Roth* [140] in the 1964 *Jacobellis* [141] decision. While recognizing the necessity for preventing the distribution of "material deemed harmful to children," the Court did not feel it necessitated withholding such materials from adults. [142] Justice Brennan and Chief Justice Warren disagreed on a major point in the opinion. Justice Brennan envisaged a national standard for obscenity while Justice Warren supported a community standard. The ruling in *Jacobellis* [143] and a 1966 ruling in *Memoirs* [144] supporting a three-fold test for obscenity were harbingers of five landmark cases in 1973 which have affected censorship legislation since that date.

In 1968 *Ginsberg* [145] provided the Court with an opportunity to postulate concerning materials that are not obscene with respect to adults but which may be prohibited for minors. At issue was the New York state statute preventing

---

140. Roth v. United States, 354 U.S. 476, 77 S.Ct. 1304, 1 L. Ed. 2d 1498 (1957).

141. Jacobellis v. Ohio, 378 U.S. 184, 84 S. Ct. 1676, 12 L. Ed. 2d 793 (1964).

142. *Ibid.*, p. 195.

143. *Ibid.*

144. Book Named "John Cleland's Memoirs of a Woman of Pleasure" v. Attorney General, 383 U.S. 413, 86 S.Ct. 975, 16 L. Ed. 2d 1 (1966); the five cases were Paris Adult Theatre I v. Slaton, 413 U.S. 49, 93 S. Ct. 2628, 37 L. Ed. 2d 446 (1973); Kaplan v. California, 413 U.S. 115, 93 S. Ct. 2680, 37 L. Ed. 2d 492 (1973); United States v. 12 200-Ft. Reels of Super 8mm. Film, 413 U.S. 123, 93 S. Ct. 2665, 37 L. Ed. 2d 500 (1973); United States v. Orito, 413 U.S. 139, 93 S. Ct. 2674, 37 L. Ed. 2d 513 (1973); and Miller v. California, 413 U.S. 15, 93 S. Ct. 2607, 37 L. Ed. 2d 419 (1973).

145. Ginsberg v. New York, 390 U.S. 629, 88 S. Ct. 1274, 20 L. Ed. 2d 195 (1968).

the dissemination of "girlie" magazines to juveniles under the age of seventeen. The Supreme Court with Justice William Brennan writing the majority opinion upheld the New York statute, thus distinguishing between material held not obscene for adults but harmful for minors. It should be pointed out that *Ginsberg* [146] required the three-fold test as decided in *Roth*. [147] To be declared obscene the material must be proved to be: (1) appealing to the prurient interest; (2) patently offensive; and (3) lacking in redeeming social importance. [148] Objectionable material must satisfy the *Roth* standard before such could be proscribed for minors.

The Supreme Court's *Ginsberg* [149] decision was not a First Amendment rights homily applicable to minors versus adults. It was a juvenile obscenity decision. The Court insisted the New York statute which prohibited sale or distribution of obscene materials to juveniles was constitutional. If materials were sold to minors, they must be assessed on the basis of the influence of prurient interest on juveniles.

On June 21, 1973, the Supreme Court handed down a new set of guidelines that in effect enabled states to ban material offensive as determined by local standards. [150] The Court's *Miller* [151] decision is the most significant. For the first time since the 1966 *Memoirs* [152] case, the Supreme

---

146. *Ibid.*

147. Roth v. United States, 354 U.S. 476, 77 S. Ct. 1304, 1 L. Ed. 2d 1498 (1957).

148. *Ibid.*

149. Ginsberg v. New York, supra note 145.

150. Paris Adult Theatre I v. Slaton, supra note 144; Kaplan v. California, supra note 144; United States v 12 200-Ft. Reels, supra note 144; United States v. Orito, supra note 144; and Miller v. California, supra note 144.

151. Miller v. California, supra note 144.

152. Book Named "John Cleland's Memoirs of a Woman of Pleasure" v. Attorney General, supra note 144.

Court focused on an actual definition of obscenity.

> This case involves the application of a State's criminal obscenity statute to a situation in which sexually explicit materials have been thrust by aggressive sales action upon unwilling recipients who had in no way indicated any desire to receive such materials.[153]

The five cases were all decided by a five to four margin. Chief Justice Warren Burger wrote the majority opinions and was joined by Justices Harry Blackmun, Lewis F. Powell, Jr., William H. Rehnquist, and Byron R. White. The *Miller*[154] decision established a three-fold test to determine obscenity:

> (a) whether "the average person, applying contemporary community standards" would find that the work, taken as a whole, appeals to the prurient interest . . . (b) whether the work depicts or describes, in a patently offensive way, sexual conduct specifically defined by the applicable state law, and (c) whether the work taken as a whole, lacks serious artistic, political, or scientific value.[155]

This attempt at clarifying the definition of obscenity has been of little help to lower courts. Justice William O. Douglas' dissenting opinion in *Roth*[156] raised the questions that have troubled those involved in censorship litigation since *Roth* and *Miller*.[157]

> Any test that turns on what is offensive to the community's standards is too loose, too capricious, too destructive of freedom of expression to be squared with the First Amendment. Under that test, juries can censor,

---

153. Miller v. California, supra note 144, p. 18.

154. *Ibid.*

155. *Ibid.*, p. 24.

156. Roth v. United States, 354 U.S. 476, 77 S. Ct. 1304, 1 L. Ed. 2d 1498 (1957).

157. *Ibid.*, p. 1322.

suppress, and punish what they don't like, provided the matter relates to "sexual impurity" or has a tendency "to excite lustful thoughts." This is community censorship in one of its worst forms. It creates a regime where in the battle between the literati and the Philistines, the Philistines are certain to win.[158]

Questions arising from the *Miller* decision have not been answered. Who is the "average person?" Who defines "contemporary community standards?" What will be the impact of the decisions? Until the jury renders a decision, the librarian and the school administrator cannot be sure.

Confusion has resulted for school systems facing litigation in matters of censorship concerning school library and instructional materials. The attention of the community seems to have turned away from hard-core pornography or adult book stores and toward public schools.

The fifty-state General Assemblies are empowered to permutate obscenity statutes based on community standards established in *Miller.* If the obscenity statute is litigated then it becomes the responsibility of federal judges and/or juries to square the legislation and community standards with the Constitution.

§ 3.3. Censorship Cases.

A. CASES SUPPORTING SCHOOL BOARD ACTION.

In *Parker,*[159] a probationary teacher in Prince George's County, Maryland, alleged he was dismissed and his contract terminated in violation of First, Fifth, and Fourteenth Amendment rights.[160] Justice Thompson writing the opinion insisted the board had simply not

---

158. *Ibid.*
159. Parker v. Board of Educ., 237 F. Supp. 222 (D. Md.), *aff'd,* 348 F.2d 464 (4th Cir. 1965), *cert. denied,* 382 U.S. 1030 (1966).
160. *Ibid.,* p. 224.

101

renewed the contract. School board policies maintained that contracts of non-tenured teachers could be terminated by written notice at end of the first or second year before tenure was acquired.

Plaintiff claimed his contract was terminated because he assigned Aldous Huxley's *Brave New World* in a psychology class. In the curriculum guide for the course, *Brave New World* was listed as optional or selected reading rather than required reading.

The school board maintained that Parker's contract was not renewed because his "approach to teaching" and "method of handling students were not suitable at the senior high school level." [161] Furthermore, plaintiff was unwilling to follow outlined procedures in assigning reading.

Justice Thompson acknowledged that *Brave New World* was not an issue in the case. Even if it were, said Justice Thompson, the "right of free speech or expression like other First Amendment guarantees is not absolute." [162] Finally, Justice Thompson insisted that the school board had the privilege of refusing to renew non-tenured teachers' contracts.

In the *Medeiros* [163] case parents of fifth and sixth public school grade students protested the use of a film series in a newly adopted family life and sex education curriculum. Plaintiff-parents contended the program was an invasion of privacy and a violation of religious freedom. The films consisted of fifteen lessons covering "interpersonal relations, self-understanding, family structure and sex education." [164] Lessons eleven through fifteen concerned sexual

---

161. *Ibid.*
162. *Ibid.,* p. 229.
163. Medeiros v. Kiyosaki, 52 Hawaii 436, 478 P.2d 314 (1970).
164. *Ibid.,* p. 315.

development and sexuality. The films were designed for use on educational television. When the State Department of Education adopted the program an "excusal system" was included. Parents or guardians who objected on moral or religious grounds could have their children excused. Thus, the program was not compulsory.

Plaintiffs cited *Meyer*[165] and *Pierce*[166] to support their invasion of privacy contention. The court with Justice Richardson writing the opinion held that the two decisions were supportive of freedom of speech rather than privacy. Moreover, insisted Justice Richardson, parents' right of privacy had not been violated.

Justice Richardson next addressed the issue of First Amendment freedom of religion violation. Since the program was not compulsory, Justice Richardson maintained there was not "any direct or substantial burden on their 'free exercise' of religion."[167]

Plaintiffs further argued that the program was illegal because the State Department of Education must have specific authorization from the legislature to adopt programs. Justice Richardson recognized the adoption of sex education programs was within the jurisdiction of the State Department of Education. Moreover, the program had been adopted by the school board. Justice Richardson insisted that it was proper for the school district to continue the sex education program.

The *Presidents Council*[168] decision was the first case concerning a local school board's authority denying use of

---

165. Meyer v. Nebraska, 262 U.S. 390, 43 S. Ct. 625, 67 L. Ed. 1042 (1923).

166. Pierce v. Society of Sisters of the Holy Names of Jesus and Mary, 268 U.S. 510, 45 S. Ct. 571, 69 L. Ed. 1070 (1925).

167. Medeiros v. Kiyosaki, supra note 163.

168. Presidents Council, Dist. 25 v. Community School Bd. No. 25, 457 F.2d 289 (2d Cir.), *cert. denied,* 409 U.S. 998 (1972).

specific books the board deemed inappropriate for students.[169] As previously stated, federal courts have been reluctant to intervene in such matters unless constitutional issues are directly implicated.[170] The New York Legislature empowers the school boards with the responsibility of library book selection.[171]

In the *Presidents Council*[172] case, the school board passed a resolution requiring the withdrawal of Piri Thomas' book *Down These Mean Streets* from junior high school libraries in the school district. Later, the school board modified the resolution by retaining the book and making it available to students by direct loan to parents. Moreover, teachers were not forbidden to discuss or assign the book which vividly describes life in New York's Spanish Harlem.

Plaintiffs in the case were past and present presidents of various parent-teacher associations (Presidents Council), students, parents, teachers, a librarian, and a principal. Plaintiffs asserted that the book withdrawal violated First Amendment rights.[173] Relying on *Ginsberg*[174] plaintiffs argued that unless the book was obscene, minors have

---

169. M. David Alexander, "First Amendment: Curriculum, Libraries, and Textbooks," in *School Law in Contemporary Society,* ed. M. A. McGhehy (Topeka, Kansas: National Organization of Legal Problems of Education, 1980), p. 155.

170. Epperson v. Arkansas, 393 U.S. 97, 89 S. Ct. 266, 21 L. Ed. 2d 228 (1968).

171. New York Education Law, Consol. Laws, C. 16 2590-e (3) (McKinney 1970).

172. Presidents Council, Dist. 25 v. Community School Bd. No. 25, supra note 168.

173. *Ibid.,* p. 290.

174. Ginsberg v. New York, 390 U.S. 629, 88 S. Ct. 1274, 20 L. Ed. 2d 195 (1968).

unqualified First Amendment rights to access.[175] The court with Justice Mulligan writing the opinion chose not to accept plaintiffs' interpretation.

The plaintiffs did not question authority of the school board to select books; however, once a book had been selected, plaintiff argued, it could not be removed simply because of school board's taste or disdain for the content. Shelving a book in the school library elevated students' rights to use the book to a constitutional level. Justice Mulligan disagreed and insisted that books do not receive "tenure." The same school board authorized to select was also authorized to remove books and materials from the school library.[176]

Justice Mulligan also rejected plaintiffs' reliance on *Tinker*.[177] Plaintiffs argued that use of the book did not cause substantive or material disruption in the school. Justice Mulligan acknowledged that shelving and discarding books is a constant process based on educational, budgetary, and architectural considerations.

> To suggest that the shelving or unshelving of books presents a constitutional issue, particularly where there is no showing of freedom of speech or thought, is a proposition we cannot accept.[178]

Justice Mulligan found for the school board, finding no impingement upon any basic constitutional values in the school board's action.[179]

---

175. Presidents Council, Dist. 25 v. Community School Bd. No. 25, 457 F. 2d 289, 292 (2d Cir.), *cert. denied,* 409 U.S. 998 (1972).

176. *Ibid.,* p. 293.

177. Tinker v. Des Moines Indep. Community School Dist., 393 U.S. 503, 89 S. Ct. 733, 21 L. Ed. 2d 731 (1969).

178. Presidents Council, Dist. 25 v. Community School Bd. No. 25, supra note 175, p. 293.

179. *Ibid.,* p. 291.

The Supreme Court denied certiorari in *Presidents Council*,[180] with Justices Stewart and Douglas dissenting. Justice Douglas expressed constitutional concern in his dissenting opinion: "The First Amendment involves not only the right to speak and publish, but also the right to hear, to learn, and to know." [181]

In the 1972 *Todd*[182] decision parents brought action against the school board maintaining that use of *Slaughterhouse-Five*[183] in an elective high school current literature course violated First and Fourteenth Amendment rights because the book made reference to religious matters.[184] A Michigan trial court, with Justice Arthur Moore writing the opinion, ruled that the book must be removed from the school library. Moreover, said Justice Moore, the book should not be fostered, promoted, or recommended for use in the school system. Further, insisted Justice Moore, the book should be banned from the school library long enough to prevent its use as recommended and/ or promoted reading in the courses of study. When the school system ceased promotion or recommendation in courses, the book could be returned to library shelves.[185]

Justice Moore relied solely on *Schempp*[186] in reaching the decision. The Michigan Court of Appeals rejected Justice Moore's decision and insisted that *Schempp* was not applicable in this case.

---

180. Presidents Council, Dist. 25 v. Community School Bd. No. 25, 409 U.S. 998 (1972).

181. *Ibid.*, p. 999.

182. Todd v. Rochester Community Schools, 41 Mich. App. 320, 200 N.W.2d 90 (Mich. 1972).

183. Kurt Vonnegut, Jr., *Slaughterhouse-Five* (New York: Delacorte Press, Inc., 1969).

184. Todd v. Rochester Community Schools, supra note 182, p. 91.

185. *Ibid.*, p. 94.

186. School Dist. of Abington Township v. Schempp, 374 U.S. 203, 83 S. Ct. 1560, 10 L. Ed. 2d 844 (1963).

Although Justice Moore never declared that *Slaughterhouse-Five* was obscene, he suggested the possibility.[187] The Court of Appeals, with Justice Bronson writing the opinion, maintained that the book was clearly not obscene under any constitutional test. Furthermore, Justice Bronson chastised the lower court for imposing its own value judgment on citizenry, the "trial court abused its discretion in entering this traditionally sacred area." [188] Justice Bronson insisted:

> Our Constitution will tolerate no supreme censor nor allow any man to superimpose his judgment on that of others so that the latter are denied freedom to decide and choose for themselves.[189]

Aside from the matter of obscenity, Justice Bronson maintained that use of the novel for literary reasons did not violate the First Amendment establishment of religion clause. Although public schools may not teach religion, they may teach about religion. Plaintiff's constitutional theory was impermissible. Finally, Justice Bronson issued a strong statement in favor of freedom of expression:

> If plaintiff's contention was correct, then public school students could no longer marvel at Sir Galahad's saintly quest for the Holy Grail, nor be introduced to the dangers of Hitler's *Mein Kampf* nor read the mellifluous poetry of John Milton and John Donne. Unhappily, Robin Hood would be forced to forage without Friar Tuck and Shakespeare would have to delete Shylock from *The Merchant of Venice.* Is this to be the state of our law? Our Constitution does not command ignorance; on the contrary, it assures the people that the state may not relegate them to such a

---

187. Todd v. Rochester Community Schools, supra note 182, p. 97.
188. *Ibid.*, p. 97.
189. *Ibid.*, p. 98.

status and guarantees to all the precious and unfettered freedom of pursuing one's own intellectual pleasures in one's own personal way.[190]

Judgment against the school board was reversed.

In the 1972 *Lindros*[191] case, a probationary teacher brought action against Torrance Unified School District school board seeking to have the decision not to rehire him reversed. The Los Angeles Superior Court sustained the school board's action.

Lindros, the appellant, was a tenth-grade English teacher. He gave his students an assignment to write a short story relating to an emotional and personal experience. *Lindros* varied from *Keefe*[192] and *Parducci*.[193] In response to a request from some students, the teacher read to his five classes his own original composition, a short story entitled "The Funeral." The short story ended with a vulgar term. In one or more classes he read the full expression. Lindros contended that refusal to rehire him because he read "The Funeral" violated his academic freedom protected by the First Amendment. Appellant grounded his judicial logic in the reasoning of *Parducci*[194] and *Keefe*.[195] The short story was: (1) not obscene; (2) the slang words were common in usuage; and (3) the story had a definite literary purpose. There had been no student or parent complaints. Moreover, works with similar words could be found elsewhere in the school curriculum. And also, students were required to attend plays where similar words were used. No

---

190. *Ibid.*, p. 93.
191. Lindros v. Governing Bd., 108 Cal. Rptr. 185, 9 Cal. 3d 524, 510 P.2d 361 (1973).
192. Keefe v. Geanakos, 418 F.2d 359 (1st Cir. 1969).
193. Parducci v. Rutland, 316 F. Supp. 352 (D.C. Ala. 1970).
194. *Ibid.*
195. Keefe v. Geanakos, supra note 192.

material classroom disruption resulted. Finally Lindros said, "To allow a teacher not to be rehired for such teaching would chill free speech and stifle creative teaching innovation."[196]

The court with Justice Forel writing the opinion insisted that "academic freedom does not signify the absence of all restraint." Citing *Mailloux*,[197] Justice Forel distinguished between the secondary school and college.

> The faculty in secondary schools does not have the independent traditions, the broad discretion as to teaching methods, nor usually the intellectual qualifications, of university professors. Among secondary school teachers there are often many persons with little experience. Some teachers and most students have limited intellectual and emotional maturity.

In contrasting *Keefe*,[198] the case in that instance involved the reading of a scholarly, thought-provoking article supplied by the department. Propriety or impropriety of offensive language depends on the circumstances of use. In *Keefe* the students were in twelfth grade and the use of vulgar language served a legitimate, professional purpose. In *Lindros* [199] the students were tenth graders. Use of vulgarity in a story used as a model "substantially transcended any legitimate professional purpose and was without the pale of academic freedom."[200] Lindros' action carried with it the probability of adverse effect on the welfare of students.

---

196. Lindros v. Governing Bd., supra note 191, p. 193.

197. Mailloux v. Kiley, 323 F. Supp. 1387 (D. Mass.), *aff'd,* 448 F.2d 1242 (1st Cir. 1971).

198. Keefe v. Geanakos, supra note 192.

199. Lindros v. Governing Bd., supra note 191.

200. *Ibid.*, p. 195.

The fact of the reading of "The Funeral" to classes was sufficient cause not to rehire Lindros.[201]

In the 1974 *Brubaker*[202] case three non-tenured eighth grade teachers were notified that their contracts would not be renewed the following year. Clara Brubaker taught French, John Brubaker taught industrial arts, and Ronald Sievert taught language arts. Sievert had received notice that his contract would be renewed for one year only. As a matter of fact all three teachers were dismissed before completion of the school term for distributing in the school a promotional brochure for an "R"-rated movie, *Woodstock*. A particular poem "Getting Together" published in the brochure was the irritating point:

> [R]eferred to apparent joys of smoking marijuana and . . . invited children to throw off discipline imposed on them by the moral environment of their homelife and enter a new world of love and freedom.[203]

Parents complained that two of the teachers made the brochures available to eighth-grade students. The third teacher was implicated for bringing the material to the school.

---

201. *Ibid.*

202. Brubaker v. Board of Educ., 502 F.2d 973 (7th Cir. 1974).

203. *Ibid.*, p. 973. Those parts of "Getting Together" relating to drugs, sexual behavior and what might be called vulgarities are as follows:

> Woodstock felt like home. A place to take acid. A place to make love . . . But now it's all now, and it feels like we're never turning back.
> Woodstock felt like a swell of energy, wave of elation that fills the heart and flows on over the lover beside you . . .
> Oh joy overflowing, oh lover caressing, I am what I have to share, oh take me completely!
> Grass smoked together. Stink of our shit; Music of Laughter . . . Bodies naked into the water, touching each other, opening hearts into greater awareness of being together . . . moving together we're a big fucking wave . . .! Its only the beginning . . .
> Old world crumbling, new world being born.

Ibid., pp. 975-76.

The school board declared the materials "obscene and of a suggestive nature." [204] Further, the school board insisted the material subjected students to a viewpoint contrary to requirements of Illinois state law. The law in question concerned teaching about the harmful effects of alcohol and narcotics.

Plaintiffs complained that dismissal abridged civil rights under the First and Fourteenth Amendments. They further alleged that the school board had breached contracts and had defamed them. The Brubakers and Sievert petitioned for back pay and attorneys' fees on procedural due process grounds.

The federal district court affirmed dismissal upholding the school board on all counts. On appeal the Seventh Circuit Court of Appeals with Justice O'Sullivan writing the opinion insisted that the school board's action was not arbitrary or capricious and was not a violation of First Amendment rights. Relying on *Paris Adult Theatre,* [205] dicta Justice O'Sullivan maintained that expert testimony was not required when alleged obscene material was introduced in evidence.

Appellants argued they were not aware of the state statute concerning teaching effects of alcoholic drinks and narcotics. Justice O'Sullivan asserted that regardless of knowledge of the law, "teachers should have known better than to hand to their young students something that invited use of the described drugs." [206]

Relying on *Mailloux,*[207] Justice O'Sullivan insisted:

---

204. *Ibid.,* p. 975.

205. Paris Adult Theatre I v. Slaton, 413 U.S. 49, 93 S. Ct. 2628, 37 L. Ed. 2d 446 (1973).

206. Brubaker v. Board of Educ., supra note 202, p. 984.

207. Mailloux v. Kiley, 323 F. Supp. 1387 (D. Mass.), *aff'd,* 448 F.2d 1242 (1st Cir. 1971).

it did not intend . . . to do away with what, to use an old fashioned term, are considered the properties, or to give carte blanche in the name of academic freedom to conduct which can reasonably be deemed both offensive and unnecessary to the accomplishment of educational objectives.[208]

Moreover, continued Justice O'Sullivan, consideration must always be given to educational purpose, age, and sophistication of students. Likewise, purpose and relevance of material and the manner of presentation must also be taken into account.[209]

There were no First Amendment and/or otherwise civil rights violations determined in the case. Justice O'Sullivan rejected back pay and attorneys' fees for appellants since dismissal was for just cause.

In the 1977 *Cary*[210] case five high school English teachers brought action against the Adams-Arapahoe County school board because the board disqualified ten books, which teachers had been using, from a list of 1,275 approved textbooks. In a legal sense the books were not obscene and neither did they represent a specific ideology or philosophy. The school board had appointed a book reviewing committee and the committee recommended that nine books be rejected. The school board rejected ten.[211]

Plaintiffs alleged that removal of the books was a violation of the First and Fourteenth Amendments. Plaintiffs insisted that school board action was really a form of prior restraint.[212] In the initial 1977 Federal District Court deci-

208. Brubaker v. Board of Educ., supra note 202, 984-85.

209. *Ibid.*, p. 985.

210. Cary v. Board of Educ., Slip Opinion Nos. 77-1297, 77-1298 (10th Cir. 1979).

211. Cary v. Board of Educ., 427 F. Supp. 945, 947 (D. Colo. 1977), *aff'd,* 598 F.2d 535 (10th Cir. 1979).

212. *Ibid.*, p. 949.

sion, Justice Richard Matsch maintained that teachers' book selection was protected by the First Amendment.[213] Yet, Justice Matsch insisted that the constitutional issue was spoiled by a collective bargaining contract between teachers and school board. Justice Matsch maintained that by signing the contract teachers in effect had surrendered individual professional rights.[214] Otherwise, acknowledged Justice Matsch, teachers' rights would have prevailed.

The Tenth Circuit Court of Appeals with Justice Logan writing the opinion paid close attention to the suggested flawed constitutional element and maintained that the district court erred.[215] The collective bargaining agreement, suggested Justice Logan, had given the school board control over curriculum only in so far as the contract was consistent with the constitutions of Colorado and the United States. Individual constitutional rights of teachers had not been waived.

Teachers' rights and school board authority must always be balanced, said Justice Logan. Moreover, discussion of the rejected books was not prohibited in classrooms and this was a very important feature, suggested Justice Logan.[216]

Finally, plaintiffs agreed that school board had authority to prescribe curriculum. However, plaintiffs insisted that school board members' personal taste and/or philosophies should not influence teachers' use and/or selection of instructional materials.[217] Justice Logan disagreed.[218]

Justice Logan, in sustaining school board position, acknowledged that a school board may select and remove instructional materials from the curriculum.[219]

---

213. *Ibid.*, p. 953.
214. *Ibid.*, p. 955.
215. Cary v. Board of Educ., supra note 210, p. 8.
216. *Ibid.*, p. 9.
217. *Ibid.*, p. 16.
218. *Ibid.*, p. 18.
219. *Ibid.*, p. 19.

In *Bicknell*[220] a school board was challenged for removal of books from the high school library. The two books removed were: Richard Price's *The Wanderers*—school board members believed the book was "vulgar and obscene," and Patrick Mann's *Dog Day Afternoon* which was placed in the principal's office pending establishment of a "restricted" shelf in the library. Patrick Mann's book was criticized for violence and vulgarity.

Plaintiffs argued that students' rights of free speech and due process were violated by removal and restricted use of the books. Although Justice Albert Coffin, writing the court's opinion, did not agree with the school board's action, he, in relying on *Presidents Council,*[221] insisted that school board's policies and actions did not directly infringe on the constitutional rights of students. Perhaps, the distinction between *Presidents Council*[222] and *Bicknell*[223] is not "constitutionally meaningful."

Justice Coffin determined that due process rights of students extended only to liberty and property interest of the state and federal constitutions.[224] Students have no constitutional right to use library books, insisted Justice Coffin. Moreover, students could obtain the books from other libraries. Likewise, students were not forbidden to bring the books to school or to discuss them during school hours. Finally, Justice Coffin maintained that no constitutional right had been abridged. On appeal the Second Circuit Court of Appeals with Justice Newman writing

---

220. Bicknell v. Vergennes Union High School Bd. of Directors, 475 F. Supp. 615 (D. Vt. 1979), *aff'd,* 638 F.2d 438 (2d Cir. 1980).

221. Presidents Council, Dist. 25 v. Community School Bd. No. 25, 457 F.2d 289 (2d Cir.), *cert. denied,* 409 U.S. 998 (1972).

222. *Ibid.*

223. Bicknell v. Vergennes, supra note 220.

224. David Alexander, "First Amendment," in *School Law in Contemporary Society,* p. 169.

the opinion insisted that: (1) school board's book removal created no First Amendment violation; (2) no due process hearing was necessary before book(s) removal; and (3) the school librarian had no due process consideration in light of the fact that school board took no adverse action against her — "merely removed certain functions from the job assignment." [225]

In the 1979 *Zykan* [226] case, high school students and former high school students filed a complaint against the school board for eliminating courses from the curriculum, removing books from the library and the English curriculum and failing to rehire certain English teachers. Much of the subject matter in the books and curriculum appear to deal with feminism. Justice Allen Sharp writing the court's opinion based the decision on *Brubaker*.[227] In dismissing the case for "lack of subject matter — jurisdiction" [228] Justice Sharp insisted that school boards have the authority to determine what curriculum, library books, and textbooks should be used that inculcate values of American citizenship.

On appeal the Seventh Circuit Appeals Court, Justice Cummings writing the opinion, insisted that while the district court decision was correct insofar as the case at bar at the particular time "the case was not moot." [229] In light of the new English curriculum adoption the school board had requested dismissal of the case. Yet, suggested Justice

---

225. Bicknell v. Vergennes Union High School Bd. of Directors, 638 F.2d 438 (2d Cir. 1980).

226. Zykan v. Warsaw Community School Corp., (N.D. Ind. No. s79-68, December 10, 1979).

227. Brubaker v. Board of Educ., 502 F.2d 973 (7th Cir. 1974).

228. Zykan v. Warsaw Community School Corp., 631 F.2d 1300 (7th Cir. 1980).

229. *Ibid.*, p. 1304.

Cummings, "the facts alleged and relief sought in the complaint easily survive the Board's change in curriculum." [230] Thus, Justice Cummings vacated the lower court's decision and remanded with instructions:

> Nevertheless, the articulation of the principles at issue here is sufficiently novel and important that plaintiffs should be given leave to amend their complaint again, if they can, to allege the kind of interference with secondary school academic freedom that has been found to be cognizable as a constitutional claim.[231]

Finally, even though school board was not entirely successful in having the case mooted, the school board nonetheless received a victory of sorts. Justice Cummings recognized the difficulty facing plaintiffs: (1) by suggesting that thus far there was no subject matter "jurisdiction"; and (2) that plaintiffs may once again try to "amend their complaint ... if they can." [232] This suggests a tough judicial scrimmage on remand.

B. CASES SUPPORTING CONSTITUTIONAL RIGHTS.

In September, 1969, a tenured English teacher in the public schools of Ipswich, Massachusetts, assigned an article from *Atlantic Monthly* magazine to a senior English class.[233] The teacher discussed the article and explained the origin and context of an offensive word contained in the article. Moreover, the teacher explained the author's reason for including the word and stated that any student finding the assignment distasteful could receive an alternative one. The teacher was suspended with the possibility of being discharged.[234]

---

230. *Ibid.*, p. 1308.

231. *Ibid.*

232. *Ibid.*, p. 1309.

233. Keefe v. Geanakos, 305 F. Supp. 1091 (D. Mass), *rev'd and remanded*, 418 F.2d 359 (1st Cir. 1969).

234. *Ibid.*

116

The First Circuit Court of Appeals in *Keefe* [235] found the article not pornographic but "scholarly, thoughtful, and thought-provoking." [236] Justice Aldrich, writing the court's opinion, insisted that no proper discussion of the article could avoid consideration of the vulgar term because it was important to the development of the article's thesis.

Justice Aldrich indicated that whether or not offensive language is constitutionally protected depends on the circumstances. Although Justice Aldrich agreed with defendants that obscenity standards for students could not be determined by those assumed for adults, the decision insisted that a "high school senior is not devoid of all discrimination or resistance." [237] Continuing, Justice Aldrich maintained:

> Hence the question in this case is whether a teacher may, for demonstrated educational purposes, quote a "dirty" word currently used in order to give special offense, or whether the shock is too great for high school seniors to stand. If the answer is that the students must be protected from such exposure we would fear for their future. We do not question the good faith of the defendants in believing that some parents have been offended. With the greatest of respect to such parents, their sensibilities are not the full measure of what is proper education.[238]

The *Keefe* [239] decision acknowledged that academic freedom based on the First Amendment is basic to a democratic society and has judicial protection. And as in *Keefe*,[240] a federal court ruled in *Parducci* [241] that teachers' First

---

235. *Ibid.*
236. *Ibid.*
237. *Ibid.*, p. 360.
238. *Ibid.*, pp. 361-62.
239. *Ibid.*
240. *Ibid.*
241. Parducci v. Rutland, 316 F. Supp. 352 (M.D. Ala. 1970).

Amendment right to use controversial material or language must be constitutionally protected unless school officials can establish that: (1) it is irrelevant to subject matter being taught; (2) it is disruptive to school discipline; and/or (3) it is inappropriate for the maturity level of students.

In the 1970 *Parducci* [242] case a first-year English teacher brought action against members of the school administration and school board of Montgomery County, Alabama. Plaintiff insisted that her dismissal for assigning Kurt Vonnegut's *Welcome to the Monkey House* to a class of high school juniors violated her First Amendment right to academic freedom. The principal and associate superintendent described the story as "literary garbage . . . with a philosophy condoning . . . killing off of elderly people and free sex." [243] Three students asked to be excused from the assignment and several parents complained to the principal.

Justice Frank Johnson, writing the court's opinion, found nothing that would render the story obscene under *Roth,* [244] nor under the stricter standards yardstick for minors in *Ginsberg.* [245] Relying on *Tinker* [246] Justice Johnson maintained that teachers are entitled to First Amendment freedoms. Moreover, constitutional protection is not affected by the presence or absence of state tenure statutes. The school system had not previously forbidden the use of the short story, and no person should be punished unless conduct has been proscribed in precise terms. Likewise, the

---

242. *Ibid.*

243. *Ibid.,* p. 353.

244. Roth v. United States, 354 U.S. 476, 77 S. Ct. 1304, 1 L. Ed. 2d 1498 (1957).

245. Ginsberg v. New York, 390 U.S. 629, 88 S. Ct. 1274, 20 L. Ed. 2d 195 (1968).

246. Tinker v. Des Moines Indep. Community School Dist., 393 U.S. 503, 89 S. Ct. 733, 21 L. Ed. 2d 731 (1969).

assignment caused no disruption among students. Under such vague standards and/or lack of standards, maintained Justice Johnson, teachers will be reluctant to experiment and investigate new and different ideas. The dismissal of Parducci insisted Justice Johnson, "constituted an unwarranted invasion of her First Amendment right to academic freedom." [247]

In the *Sterzing*[248] case, a teacher in Fort Bend, Texas was dismissed for discussing racial issues with high school students. The United States District Court for the Southern District of Texas, with Justice Carl D. Bue writing the opinion, maintained that the teacher's First and Fourteenth Amendment rights were violated. Justice Bue ordered the school district to award the teacher $20,000 in general damages, $5,000 for attorney's fees, and to expunge from the record all references to his being discharged. Justice Bue denied teacher's request for restoration to his former position "on the grounds that reinstatement would only revive antagonisms and that the award of monetary damages compensated Sterzing for his expectance of reemployment." [249] Sterzing appealed to the Fifth Circuit of Appeals on grounds that the federal district court denied his right of reemployment.

The Fifth Circuit Court of Appeals in a Per Curiam opinion insisted the lower court's judicial rationale refusing reinstatement was impermissible. Thus, the case was remanded to the lower court for reconsideration and remedy.[250]

---

247. Parducci v. Rutland, supra note 241, at p. 357.

248. Sterzing v. Fort Bend Indep. School Dist., 376 F. Supp. 657 (S.D. Tex. 1972), *vacated and remanded,* 496 F.2d 92 (5th Cir. 1974).

249. *Ibid.*

250. Sterzing v. Fort Bend Indep. School Dist., 496 F.2d 92 (5th Cir. 1972).

In the 1976 *Minarcini*[251] case five high school students brought action through parents against the Strongsville, Ohio City School District, the school board, and the superintendent. Plaintiffs claimed that withdrawal of books from the school library violated their First and Fourteenth Amendment rights.[252] The Sixth Circuit Court of Appeals disagreed with the 1972 Second Circuit Court of Appeals decision in *Presidents Council*[253] (which upheld the right of school board to remove materials from school library) and found for the students on First Amendment grounds.

The Strongsville School Board had passed a resolution removing Kurt Vonnegut's *Cat's Cradle* from libraries in the school district and to forbid its use in the classroom. At a later meeting Vonnegut's *God Bless You, Mr. Rosewater* and Joseph Heller's *Catch 22* were also banned.[254]

The Sixth Circuit Court of Appeals with Justice Edwards writing the opinion, separated textbook removal and the library book banning into different issues. Justice Edwards affirmed the lower federal district court's decision upholding the school board's authority over textbooks.[255] But, insisted Justice Edwards, neither state nor school board is required to establish libraries in schools. But once the library is established there is constituted a privilege that cannot be withdrawn because of political and social tastes. Library books were thus elevated to constitutional status and in effect had "tenure."[256] Thus, book withdrawal

---

251. Minarcini v. Strongsville City School Dist., 384 F. Supp. 698 (N.D. Ohio 1974), *aff'd in part, rev'd in part,* 541 F.2d 577 (6th Cir. 1976).

252. *Ibid.*, p. 584.

253. Presidents Council, Dist. 25 v. Community School Bd. No. 25, 457 F.2d 289 (2d Cir.), *cert. denied,* 409 U.S. 998 (1972).

254. Minarcini v. Strongsville City School Dist., supra note 251, pp. 577-78.

255. *Ibid.*, p. 582.

256. *Ibid.*, p. 583.

would violate First Amendment rights of students. Justice Edwards insisted that book banning was a more serious violation of students' rights than the prohibition of wearing armbands in *Tinker.*[257] Clearly, acknowledged Justice Edwards, students' rights had been violated.

Finally, Justice Edwards addressed the critical issue of students' right to receive information. Justice Edwards alluded to the important Supreme Court quote in *Virginia State Board of Pharmacy*:

> We acknowledged that this court has referred to a First Amendment right to "receive information and ideas," and that freedom of speech "necessarily protects the right to receive." [258]

Thus, insisted Justice Edwards, once library books are placed on the shelf they can be removed only for constitutionally allowable reasons.[259] *Minarcini* was the first school censorship case to uphold students' right to receive information.

There is yet another side of book banning that should be explored. The conflict occurs when a teacher makes a professional judgement in selection and utilization of reading material that collides with the administration's judgement. The dichotomy becomes intuitively obvious—the teacher is dismissed for insubordination. The 1977 *Harris*[260] case is a good example.

During the 1973 school year, Harris, an English teacher with nine years' experience, used J. D. Salinger's novel,

---

257. Tinker v. Des Moines Indep. Community School Dist., 393 U.S. 503, 89 S. Ct. 733, 21 L. Ed. 2d 731 (1969).

258. Virginia State Bd. of Pharmacy v. Virginia Citizens Consumer Council, Inc., 425 U.S., p. 757.

259. Minarcini v. Strongsville, supra note 251, p. 583.

260. Harris v. Mechanicsville Central School Dist., 394 N.Y.S.2d 302 (1977).

Catcher in the Rye, in a sophomore English class. The teacher had for many years used the novel. But 1973 was to be different. Early in the 1973 school year many parents complained about the method the teacher used in presenting the novel.

The superintendent held a meeting in which the teacher agreed to find a substitute for the *Catcher in the Rye.* A memorandum was circulated to that effect following the meeting. The teacher received a copy of the memorandum and did not express any objection to the contents.[261]

In 1974 the teacher again used the novel without discussion or consent of school officials. The administration convened another meeting. At this meeting the teacher walked out and refused to return upon request. He was suspended for insubordination and for violating the agreement. Subsequently, a hearing was held and Harris was dismissed for insubordination.

Harris litigated on dismissal for insubordination grounds instead of First Amendment right to use the novel and in defense of his teaching methods. There is every likelihood that if the case had been litigated on First Amendment grounds the court would have found for the teacher. Alas, though, the issue was insubordination. And even in this issue Justice Main indicated the penalty was harsh and should be modified. Nonetheless, Justice Main sustained dismissal for insubordination "what does matter is that petitioner decided to and did enter into an understanding which was later summarized and reduced to writing and furnished to petitioner." [262]

On appeal to the New York Court of Appeals Justice Breitel sustained the lower courts decision and insisted the teacher was guilty of insubordination. Yet, suggested Jus-

---

261. *Ibid.,* p. 303.

262. *Ibid.,* p. 304. See also Celestine v. Lafayette Parish School Bd., 284 So. 2d 650 (La. 1973).

tice Breitel, the insubordination charge did not include "moral delinquency or predatory motive." [263] Moreover, there was no question with respect to his ability. Thus, said Justice Breitel, "dismissal of the teacher was so disproportionate to the offense as to shock the court's sense of fairness and an appropriate sanction was, at most, one year's suspension without pay." [264]

In the 1978 *Right to Read* [265] case a Chelsea, Massachusetts parent objected to one poem in an anthology *Male and Female* used in the high school's creative writing and adolescent literature courses. The school board reviewed the poem and determined it was "filthy" and used "offensive" language and removed the book from the school library.[266] Plaintiffs were members of the Right to Read Committee who maintained that removal of the book violated First Amendment rights of students.

The court, Justice Tauro writing the opinion, rejected school board contention that the poem was obscene. Moreover, Justice Tauro rejected school board's reliance on *Presidents Council* [267] for judicial precedent since the court did not consider the book to be obsolete, irrelevant, or obscene.[268] Likewise, Justice Tauro insisted that school boards must consider First Amendment rights of students and teachers before materials are removed.[269]

---

263. Harris v. Mechanicville Cent. School Dist., 408 N.Y.S.2d 384 (1978).

264. *Ibid.*

265. Right to Read Defense Comm. v. School Committee, 454 F. Supp. 703, 707 (D. Mass. 1978).

266. *Ibid.*

267. Presidents Council, Dist. 25 v. Community School Bd. No. 25, 457 F.2d 289 (2d Cir.), *cert. denied,* 409 U.S. 998 (1972).

268. Right to Read Defense Comm. v. School Committee, supra note 265, p. 714.

269. *Ibid.*

The *Tinker* [270] dictum is the compelling force in this case. Where constitutional implications are in question the school board must demonstrate some substantial and legitimate interest for a book's removal. Personal prejudice of individual school board members is not sufficient cause.

Finally Justice Tauro relying on the judicial wisdom of the 1969 *Red Lion* [271] decision insisted that right to learn about and react to controversial ideas is protected by the First Amendment. The concept of knowing, acknowledged Justice Tauro, is vital to the concept that truth should prevail. Thus, Justice Tauro found for the plaintiffs.

The litigious issue before the court in the 1979 *Salvail* [272] case was the school board's removal of *Ms.* magazine from a high school library. Plaintiffs were a high school student, a teacher, and taxpayers.

Relying on suggested guidelines from the New Hampshire State Department of Education, the Nashua school board established a committee to draft "Guidelines for Selecting Instructional Materials." [273] Interim guidelines were put into effect whereby the school board delegated the selection of instructional materials to the professional teachers and administrative staff.

Specific procedures were set up to handle questions and complaints. An instructional Materials Reconsideration Committee made up of librarians, the principal or his representative, the appropriate assistant superintendent, the person involved in the original selection, and the person(s) using material in the particular school involved, were to be

---

270. Tinker v. Des Moines Indep. Community School Dist., 393 U.S. 503, 89 S. Ct. 733, 21 L. Ed. 2d 731 (1969).

271. Red Lion Broadcasting Co. v. Federal Communications Comm'n, 395 U.S. 367, 89 S. Ct. 1794, 23 L. Ed. 2d 371 (1969).

272. Salvail v. Nashua Bd. of Educ., 469 F. Supp. 1269 (D.N.H. 1979).

273. *Ibid.*, p. 1271.

appointed to handle complaints. The committee then was to report findings to the superintendent who would forward copies of the recommendation to the complainant. The complaining party was granted right of appeal to the superintendent. If still not satisfied, the complainant could appeal to the school board.[274]

As this story goes a school board member presented a formal resolution to remove *Ms.* magazine from the high school library. Other school board members suggested that interim guidelines be followed, and the superintendent explained procedures for review. One school board member took the position that they were not bound by interim guidelines. By a five to three vote the subscription to *Ms.* was cancelled and all issues were removed from the library.[275]

The school board member who initiated the resolution was concerned about advertisements picturing sexually oriented devices, articles dealing with witchcraft and homosexuality, and advertisements dealing with communistic materials and records. The complaining school board member suggested that a proper test, to ascertain if material should be available to high school students, was "whether it could be read aloud to his daughter in the classroom." [276]

Plaintiffs testified that material in *Ms.* was used by students to research social issues from the feminist viewpoint. Experts manifestly testified the magazine was not obscene. In the meantime, the school board had revised guidelines which would include any school board member on the reconsideration committee.[277] The school board then reexamined the magazine and returned the two issues to the library with the questionable advertisements removed.

---

274. *Ibid.*
275. *Ibid.*, p. 1272.
276. *Ibid.*
277. *Ibid.*

The court, with Justice Devine writing the opinion, and relying on the judicial philosophy developed in *Minarcini* [278] insisted that the school district is not required to provide a library for students, but once having done so the school board could not condition use based solely on social or political tastes of the board. Having adopted interim guidelines, the school board was required to follow them.

Alluding to *Virginia Pharmacy*, Justice Devine maintained that school authorities "must bear burden of showing substantial government interest to be served" in restricting information.[279]

Finally, Justice Devine determined that constitutional rights had been violated. The school board "failed to demonstrate a substantial and legitimate government interest sufficient to warrant removal of *Ms.* magazine from the Nashua High School library.[280]

In the 1982 *Sheck* [281] decision, students and their parents sought declaratory and injunctive relief restoring Ronald J. Glasser's *365 Days* to the high school library shelf. The Baileyville School Committee had removed the book because of objectionable language. Justice Cyr, writing the court's opinion, insisted that banning the entire book because of objectionable language as determined by a school committee of which two members had never read the book "entitled students and parents of students to a preliminary injunction against banning of the book." [282] The plaintiffs,

---

278. Minarcini v. Strongsville City School Dist., 384 F. Supp. 698 (N.D. Ohio 1974), *aff'd in part, rev'd in part,* 541 F.2d 577 (6th Cir. 1976).

279. Virginia State Bd. of Pharmacy v. Virginia Citizens' Consumer Council, Inc., 425 U.S. 748, 96 S. Ct. 1817, 48 L. Ed. 2d 346 (1976).

280. Salvail v. Nashua, supra note 272, p. 1275.

281. Sheck v. Baileyville School Comm., 530 F. Supp. 679 (D. Me. 1982).

282. *Ibid.,* (Ronald J. Glasser's *365 Days* is a compilation of nonfictional Vietnam War accounts by American combat soldiers.)

suggested Justice Cyr "have made a strong showing of their entitlement to interim injunctive relief." [283]

In the 1982 *Pratt* [284] decision, students and parents began a long litigious process against the Forest Lake Independent School board for deleting two films "The Lottery" and a "trailer" film from the American literature course. This story unfolds in the following manner. "The Lottery" is a short story by Shirley Jackson and the films were produced by Encyclopedia Britannica Educational Corporation. The book was not censored and remained available in the library. In February 1978, approximately fifty parents and teachers gathered for films viewing and teachers explained the importance of the films in the American literature courses. Three parents presented a formal request that the purpose of the films was (1) "the breakdown of family values and traditions"; (2) the films may cause children to question "family loyalties"; and (3) the films' senseless brutality.[285]

In March 1978, another meeting was scheduled with approximately fifty people including teachers attending. And once again the films were viewed and teachers presented reasons for using the films in the American literature course. The people attending this meeting became known as the Committee for Challenged Materials. At the conclusion of the meeting, the Challenged Committee made the following recommendations: (1) the films be discontinued at the Junior High School; and (2) that the films be included in the Senior High curriculum but parents

---

283. *Ibid.* (According to the *New York Times* and Associated Press July 18, 1982 the Baileyville School Committee voted three-two to drop efforts to censor *365 Days* and settle the case out of court. The consent decree provides for "a permanent place in the library for *365 Days*.")

284. Pratt v. Independent School Dist. No. 831, 670 F.2d 771 (8th Cir. 1982).

285. *Ibid.*

have the option to request that their children be excused from the assignment. The school board voted four to three rejecting the Challenge Committee's recommendation and subsequently voted four to three to delete the films entirely from the curriculum.[286] Plaintiffs — students and parents — initiated legal actions against the school board. The federal district court of Minnesota, with Justice Miles Lord writing the opinion, insisted "the films be restored to their prior place in the curriculum."[287] Justice Lord then provided the school board with an opportunity to justify its actions. The school board presented Justice Lord with a resolution instead of additional evidence. The school board resolution was:

> The motion picture version of "The Lottery" and the trailer film discussing the short story graphically place an exaggerated and undue emphasis on violence and bloodshed which is not appropriate or suitable for showing in a high school classroom and which has the effect of distorting the short story and overshadowing its many otherwise valuable and educationally important themes.[288]

Of course Justice Lord rejected the resolution and maintained there was no "legitimate reason for excluding the films from the curriculum."[289] The school board then appealed to the Eighth Circuit Court of Appeals. The Eighth Circuit with Justice Heaney writing the opinion, sustained the lower court's decision insisting that: (1) school board decision was predicated on "ideological and religious reasons"; and (2) such action placed restrictions on protected free speech that could not otherwise be satisfied with

---

286. *Ibid.*, p. 774.
287. *Ibid.*, p. 775.
288. *Ibid.*
289. *Ibid.*

the assumptions that the book version was still available in the library.[290] Justice Heaney said:

> The board seeks to justify its action by pointing out that the short story remains available to teachers and students in the library in printed form and a photographic recording. This fact is not decisive. Restraint on protected speech generally cannot be justified by the fact that there may be other times, places or circumstances for such expression. The symbolic effect of removing the films from the curriculum is more significant than the resulting limitation of access to the story. The board has used its official power to perform an act clearly indicating that the ideas contained in the films are unacceptable and should not be discussed or considered. This message is not lost on students and teachers, and its chilling effect is obvious.[291]

The facts, in this case at bar, are so clearly established maintained Justice Heaney. The school board policy satisfied no compelling state interest only personal "idealogical and religious" reasons. And such policy's primary effect was "for interfering with the students' rights to receive information."[292] Thus, school board decision violated students' First Amendment free speech rights.

Finally, Justice Heaney insisted that:

> What is at stake is the right to receive information and to be exposed to controversial ideas—a fundamental First Amendment right. If these films can be banned by those opposed to their ideological theme, then a precedent is set for the removal of any such work.[293]

---

290. *Ibid.*, pp. 776-78.
291. *Ibid.*, p. 779.
292. *Ibid.*
293. *Ibid.*

We close this chapter with one of the most important and recent cases. This story begins in 1975 when two school board members from the Island Tree Union Free School District attended a meeting of a conservative group, Parents of New York United (PONYU).[294] The meeting concerned objectionable books used in public schools.[295] The books were labeled by PONYU as anti-Christian, anti-Semitic, filthy, and irrelevant.[296] The Island Tree Union Free school board members checked the high school card catalog and located several of the "objectionable" books. A plea for help from school officials uncovered other books in the library and in the school curriculum.[297]

The school board appointed a committee of professionals to review the questionable books. However, recommendations of the appointed committee were not followed explicitly. Nine books were removed from the library and classrooms. The school board insisted the nine books should not be assigned as required and/or optional reading. However, the books could be discussed in class.[298]

Of course school board action was litigated. A class action suit was filed in *Pico* [299] by students, parents and friends of students alleging that students' First Amendment right was violated by the removal of books.[300]

The federal district court disallowed class action litigation, thus, students emerge as plaintiffs. Moreover, the constitutional issues were reduced to the single question of whether or not the First Amendment prohibits the

---

294. Pico v. Board of Educ., 474 F. Supp. 387 (E.D.N.Y. 1979), *rev'd and remanded,* 638 F.2d 404 (2d Cir. 1980).

295. *Ibid.*, p. 389.

296. *Ibid.*

297. *Ibid.*

298. *Ibid.*, p. 391.

299. *Ibid.*, p. 389.

300. *Ibid.*

school board from removing books from the library and curriculum.

The federal district court with Justice George C. Pratt writing the opinion rejected imperatives from *Minarcini*,[301] *Right to Read*,[302] and *Salvail*,[303] relying instead on *Presidents Council*.[304] The concept of library book "tenure"[305] and students' right to know[306] were rejected. Justice Pratt mentioned that the school board had acted within the scope of power and had not violated the constitutional rights of students.

On appeal the Second Circuit Court of Appeals with Justice Sifton writing the opinion acknowledged that there was substantial evidence suggesting that the school board was politically and religiously motivated in removing the books. Justice Sifton insisted that school board members were really less concerned with cleansing the libraries than in expressing an official policy of God and country. Moreover, teachers and pupils who ignored the policy did so at their own peril. Continuing, Justice Sifton maintained that school board administration of the policy was as much to be feared as the policy itself. Finally, Justice Sifton insisted that board policies irrespective of school board explanation "were simply pretexts for the supression of free speech."[307] In reality, the book(s) conflicting ideology—shocking the

---

301. Minarcini v. Strongsville City School Dist., 384 F. Supp. 698 (N.D. Ohio 1974), aff'd in part, rev'd in part, 541 F.2d 577 (6th Cir. 1976).

302. Right to Read Defense Comm. v. School Comm., 454 F. Supp. 703 (D. Mass. 1978).

303. Salvail v. Nashua Bd. of Educ., 469 F. Supp. 1269 (D.N.H. 1979).

304. Presidents Council, Dist. 25 v. Community School Bd. No. 25, 457 F.2d 289 (2d Cir.), cert. denied, 409 U.S. 998 (1972).

305. Minarcini v. Strongsville, supra note 301, p. 583.

306. Virginia State Bd. of Pharmacy v. Virginia Citizens' Consumers Council, Inc., 425 U.S. 748, 96 S. Ct. 1817, 48 L. Ed. 2d 346 (1976).

307. Pico v. Board of Educ., 638 F.2d 404 (2d Cir. 1981).

conscience and jarring the emotions — issues never became part of the discussion. Thus, the district court decision was reversed and the case remanded for trial.

However, instead of making the short direct route on "remand" the school board appealed the Second Circuit Court's decision to the United States Supreme Court. On October 12, 1981, the Supreme Court agreed to hear the case. And on June 25, 1982, the Supreme Court (in a five-four decision) with Justice William Brennan writing the Court's judgement affirmed the Second Circuit Court of Appeals decision. Justices Marshall, Stevens, Blackmun, and White concurred with Justice Brennan to form the majority.[308]

Justice Brennan acknowledged in the judgement that this issue was a limited one. The case did not involve textbooks and/or books with assigned readings, no imposed curriculum limitation, no classroom intrusion and/or compulsory courses, and the constitutional question did not involve the acquisition of books.

Justice Brennan insisted the only issue was library books and "the supression of ideas." [309] This case, suggested Justice Brennan, has, both substantively and procedurally, only two questions begging constitutional direction. The first question: Are there First Amendment limitations on school board discretion removing books from the school library? The second question: If the answer to the first question is in the affirmative then do the evidentiary materials suggest that school board "exceeded those limitations"? [310]

Delineating the recent Supreme Court history and juxtaposing emerging judicial philosophy emanating from

---

308. Board of Educ. v. Pico, Case No. 80-2043, 50 L.W. 4831 (1982).
309. *Ibid.*, p. 4833.
310. *Ibid.*, pp. 4834-36.

case law Justice Brennan insisted the constitution "protects the right to receive information and ideas." [311] Justice Brennan maintained that the right to receive information logically flowed from the First Amendment free speech and press and encapsulated First Amendment rights for both the "sender" to distribute literature and the right to receive such literature. This concept, acknowledged Justice Burger in his dissenting opinion, plows new constitutional ground for "no such right . . . has previously been recognized." [312] But for Justice Brennan the school library is a quiet place, dedicated to "knowledge" and "beauty." The school library is the "principal locus of . . . freedom" and a place where students voluntarily participate in self-education.[313] For Justice Brennan the school library was a special creation where the "sender" and "receiver" juxtaposed under First Amendment free speech and press. Thus, insisted Justice Brennan:

> [W]e hold that local school boards may not remove books from school library shelves simply because they dislike the ideas contained in those books and seek by their removal to "prescribe what shall be orthodox in politics, nationalism, religion, or other matters of opinion." [314]

Moreover, insisted Justice Brennan, as he addressed the evidentiary materials issue, "[w]e conclude that the materials do raise such a question." [315] Likewise, suggested Justice Brennan, the school board's "removal procedures were highly irregular and ad hoc—the antithesis of those procedures that might tend to allay suspicions regarding petitioners' motivations." [316]

---

311. *Ibid.*, p. 4835.
312. *Ibid.*, p. 4840.
313. *Ibid.*, pp. 4835-36.
314. *Ibid.*, p. 4836.
315. *Ibid.*
316. *Ibid.*, p. 4837.

Thus, the *Pico* majority acknowledges that school children not only have the right to First Amendment self-expression but also the First Amendment right to receive information and ideas. And the *Pico* majority gets especially concerned with school board members who predicate policy on personal, political and religious ideology. The *Pico* minority (Justices Burger, Powell, O'Connor, and Rehnquist) while acknowledging that school children have the right to First Amendment self-expression would grant greater responsibility to school boards in selecting library materials. The final chapter to this story was written August 13, 1982 when the Island Tree School Board voted to remove the ban on the nine questioned books and restore them to the school library. However, the books were placed on closed reserve — students may use the books with parent permission.

§ 3.4. Summary.

Three major issues have been addressed by the judiciary relative to questions concerning censorship of school library and instructional materials. They are: (1) authority of school boards in selection, removal, or restriction of materials; (2) constitutional rights of school personnel, students, and parents in selection and use of library and instructional materials; and (3) obscenity of questioned materials.

Based on an analysis of cases the trend suggests that courts most often favor school boards. In almost every censorship case, the judiciary expressed reluctance to become entangled in the day to day school operation in which school boards are vested with authority. However, when constitutional issues are in question the judiciary does not hesitate to become involved.

The litigious issues in censorship cases encapsulating conflict between school board authority and constitutional concerns are: (1) academic freedom of teachers; (2) students' right to read and receive information; (3) parents' right to direct their children's education; and (4) violation of the establishment of religion clause.

An analysis of judical decisions suggest that students' rights will prevail over parents' right to direct the education of children. In reality, parents' constitutional support received little attention in censorship cases while students' constitutional rights stand alone. Using the *Miller*[317] case as a standard, none of the cases involving the objectionable materials issue were considered obscene.

There are conflicting judicial philosophies emerging from many of the United States Circuit Courts of Appeals. These are: (1) decisions supporting school board authority were heard almost entirely in the Second Circuit; (2) decisions supporting the individual rights of students and teachers were decided within the First, Sixth, and Eighth Circuits; and (3) decisions out of the Fifth, Seventh, and Tenth Circuits suggest an even-handed approach at publication date.

The United States Supreme Court is likewise divided. There are four justices in the *Pico* majority that are concerned when school board censorship policy is predicated on personal political and religious ideological preferences. On the other horn there are four justices who make up the *Pico* minority and they would grant greater latitude to school boards in library material selection and removal. The minority reasoning is anchored in the "views of the community" concept — "elected officials express the views of their community."[318] Finally, Justice White, even though concurring in the judgement, has deferred his opinion until another day "[w]hen the findings of fact and conclusions of law are made by the district court."[319] Justice Rehnquist

---

317. Miller v. California, 413 U.S. 15, 93 S. Ct. 2607, 37 L. Ed. 2d 419 (1973).

318. Board of Educ. v. Pico, Case No. 80-2043, 50 L.W. 4831-40 (1982).

319. *Ibid.*, p. 4839.

was annoyed with Justice White's deferred action.[320] Perhaps Justice White holds the identity to future majority censorship decisions. Chapter 5 provides a more substantial discussion of these issues.

---

320. *Ibid.*, p. 4845.

Chapter 4

REVIEW OF COURT DECISIONS

§ 4.0. Introduction.
§ 4.1. Academic Freedom of Public School Teachers.
§ 4.2. Students' Rights to Read, Inquire, and Receive Information.
§ 4.3. Right of School Boards to Select and Remove Library and Instructional Materials.
§ 4.4. Parents' Right to Direct the Education of Children.

§ 4.0. Introduction.

This chapter presents a review of landmark decisions and other significant court decisions in the five categories outlined in Chapter 1. An overview is presented for each category and specific facts and judicial decisions are given. Discussion of each case is presented as it pertains to the category to which it is applied. Categories and cases are listed below:

1. Academic Freedom of Public School Teachers:
    Meyer v. Nebraska (1923).
    Keyishian v. Board of Regents (1967).
    Tinker v. Des Moines Independent Community School District (1969).
    Keefe v. Geanakos (1969).
    Parducci v. Rutland (1970).

2. Students' Right to Read, Inquire, and Receive Information:
    Tinker v. Des Moines Independent Community School District (1969).
    Virginia State Board of Pharmacy v. Virginia Citizens Consumer Council, Inc. (1976).
    Minarcini v. Strongsville City School District (1976).
    Right to Read Defense Committee of Chelsea v. School Committee of Chelsea (1978).

137

Pratt v. Independent School District No. 831 Forest Lake, Minnesota (1982).

Pico v. Board of Education, Island Tree Union Free School District (1980).

3. Right of School Boards to Select and Remove Library and Instructional Materials:

Meyer v. Nebraska (1923).

Presidents Council Dist. 25 v. Community School Board No. 25 (1972).

Minarcini v. Strongsville School District (1976).

Cary v. Board of Education of Adams-Arapahoe School District (1979).

Pico v. Board of Education, Island Tree Union Free School District (1980).

Bicknell v. Vergennes Union High School Board of Directors (1980).

4. Parents' Right to Direct the Education of Children:

Meyer v. Nebraska (1923).

Wisconsin v. Yoder (1972).

5. Religious Freedom of Public School Students as it Relates to Use of Library and Instructional Materials:

Epperson v. Arkansas (1968).

Medeiros v. Kiyosaki (1970).

Todd v. Rochester (1972).

The landmark United States Supreme Court decisions are reviewed because they pertain to constitutional rights of teachers, students, and parents. Decisions in landmark cases have established legal precedents which influence decisions related to censorship of school library and instructional materials. Other cases present decisions from various courts in the American judicial system. In several cases decisions are conflicting. Some decisions uphold the authority of school boards to select and remove library and instructional materials while other decisions place constitutional rights above school board authority in censorship cases.

§ 4.1. Academic Freedom of Public School Teachers.

Overview

Historically, recognition of academic freedom of public school teachers has moved at a snail-like pace. *Meyer, Keyishian,* and *Tinker,* the three landmark cases presented in this category, are significant in that the substance of these cases supports academic freedom for public school teachers. These cases emphasize that the compelling state interest in education and in the welfare of children must be balanced against the academic freedom of teachers. Moreover, these cases establish that professional judgement in teaching is now a judicially cognizable First Amendment right. The concept of elementary and secondary school teachers' academic freedom has supported teachers in selecting and using library and instructional materials deemed necessary by them in classroom instruction. The cases of *Geanakos* and *Parducci* are important in pointing out legal recognition of teachers' rights in censorship cases.

Meyer v. Nebraska

262 U.S. 390, 43 S. Ct.
625, 67 L. Ed. 1042 (1923)

Facts

In 1919 the State of Nebraska enacted legislation which prohibited teaching foreign languages to students below eighth grade.[1] The law applied to public, private, and parochial schools. On May 25, 1920, an instructor in Zion Parochial School was charged with teaching German to a ten-year-old child who had not yet attained the level of eighth grade. The intention of the statute was to foster the English language as the mother tongue for children of immigrants. Robert T. Meyer was found guilty by the Dis-

---

1. 1919 Neb. Laws, ch. 249.

trict Court of Hamilton County. The Supreme Court of Nebraska affirmed the judgement.

Decision

On appeal the United States Supreme Court, with Justice McReynolds writing the decision, insisted the problem was whether the statute unreasonably infringed on the liberty interest guaranteed by the Fourteenth Amendment. Justice McReynolds maintained that the legislature is subject to judicial supervision in matters concerning the proper exercise of police power. It was evident the Nebraska legislature had materially interfered with "the calling of modern language teachers, with the opportunities of pupils to acquire knowledge, and with the power of parents to control the education of their own." [2] Justice McReynolds further asserted:

> That the state may do much, go very far, indeed, in order to improve the quality of its citizens, physically, mentally, and morally, is clear; but the individual has certain fundamental rights which must be respected. The protection of the Constitution extends to all,—to those born with English on the tongue. Perhaps it would be highly advantageous if all had ready understanding of our ordinary speech, but this cannot be coerced by methods which conflict with the Constitution, — a desirable end cannot be promoted by prohibited means. [3]

The statute was declared arbitrary and not related to any justifiable end within the power of the state. Thus, the Nebraska Supreme Court judgement was reversed.

---

2. Meyer v. Nebraska, 262 U.S., p. 401.
3. *Ibid.*

Discussion

This is an early example of Supreme Court recognition that public school teachers, parents, and students have constitutional rights which must be considered by the state. The Nebraska General Assembly's political activity collided with the Fourteenth Amendment liberty interest.

The right of a teacher once employed to pursue a professional stance in his occupation was reinforced by the decision of the Supreme Court. State statutes must not inhibit this right. Justice McReynolds insisted in part:

> Plaintiff in error taught this language in school as part of his occupation. His right thus to teach and right of parents to engage him so to instruct their children, we think, are within the liberty of the Amendment. . . . Evidently the Legislature has attempted materially to interfere with the calling of modern language teachers. . . .[4]

School boards and administrators must always be aware that the Fourteenth Amendment liberty interest supports teachers' professional judgement in teaching in the classroom. School board policy and administrative rules and regulations must be established and employed in such manner that does not impede the professional process.

Keyishian v. Board of Regents of the State of New York

385 U.S. 589, 87 S. Ct. 675,
17 L. Ed. 2d 629 (1967)

Facts

Faculty members, of a once private University of Buffalo but now publicly supported, and a part of the State University of New York system, were required to sign an affidavit, called the Feinberg Certificate, which disavowed Communist membership, in order to continue employment.

---

4. *Ibid.*, p. 627.

The primary point of the Feinberg exercise was to prevent the appointment and/or retention of "subversive" faculty members. Moreover, if an employee had ever been a Communist, communication of that fact must be made to the president of the State University of New York.[5]

Three faculty members refused to sign the Feinberg Certificate and each received notice that continued refusal would lead to dismissal. A library employee, a non-faculty position, was not required to sign the Feinberg Certificate but was required to write under oath an answer to the same question. The library employee refused to do so and was dismissed. One faculty member resigned. The other two faculty members and the former library employee became appellants in litigation insisting that New York State loyalty oath statute violated the United States Constitution.

Shortly before the case went to trial the Feinberg Certificate was rescinded. Nevertheless, the hearing continued as if the "Certificate" was still mandated by statute.

Decision

In a 5-4 decision Associate Justice Brennan writing the Court's majority opinion insisted that:

1. Rescinding the Feinberg Certificate did not render moot the constitutional questions raised by plaintiffs threatened with discharge.

2. Use of the words "seditious" and "treasonable" in the New York State statute endangered academic freedom.

---

5. See Joseph E. Bryson, *Legality of Loyalty Oath and Non-Oath Requirements for Public School Teachers,* (Asheville, North Carolina: The Miller Printing Company, 1963); Joseph E. Bryson, "Academic Freedom and Due Process for Public School Teachers," *Education Horizons,* Vol. 54, No. 1, Fall, 1975.

3. New York's interest in protecting the educational system was legitimate; however, that purpose could not be pursued by means that stifled individual constitutional liberties.

4. Laws cannot be tolerated that stifle academic freedom.

5. Vagueness and/or "overbreadth" in statutes stifles individual freedom and has a "chilling effect" upon First Amendment rights.

6. The New York statute was declared unconstitutional as a First Amendment violation.

Discussion

This landmark decision nullified the infamous Feinberg Law which had continuously passed constitutional muster since the 1952 *Adler*[6] decision.

The *Keyishian* decision presents a strong statement from the Supreme Court supporting academic freedom for public school teachers. *Keyishian* has been used as a precedent in almost every public school case concerning academic freedom since it was handed down by the Court. Finally, Justice Brennan beautifully stated the Supreme Court philosophy concerning academic freedom:

> Our Nation is deeply committed to safeguarding academic freedom, which is of transcendent value to all of us and not merely to the teachers concerned. That freedom is therefore a special concern of the First Amendment, which does not tolerate laws that cast a pall of orthodoxy over the classroom. "The vigilant protection of constitutional freedoms is nowhere more vital than in the community of American schools." The classroom is peculiarly the "marketplace of ideas." The Nation's future depends upon leaders trained through wide exposure to that robust exchange of ideas which

---

6. Adler v. Board of Educ., 342 U.S. 485, 72 S. Ct. 380, 96 L. Ed. 517 (1952).

143

discovers truth "out of a multitude of tongues, [rather] than through any kind of authoritative selection." [7]

School administrators and school boards should be cognizant of First Amendment rights of teachers in making rules and regulations as well as in proscribing materials to be used in the library and classroom.

Tinker v. Des Moines Independent Community School District

393 U.S. 503, 89 S. Ct. 733,
21 L. Ed. 2d 731 (1969)

Facts

The United States Supreme Court received this case on appeal from the Eighth Circuit Court of Appeals. It involved the enforcement of a regulation prohibiting students from wearing black armbands.

In 1965 a group of Des Moines parents and students gathered together to discuss the Vietnam War and subsequently determined to publicize their objections to the Vietnam War by fasting and wearing black armbands during the Christmas holiday season. School principals became aware of the plan. During the afternoon of December 14, 1965, the school principals adopted a policy that students wearing armbands to school would be asked to remove them. If students refused to remove the armbands they would be suspended until they could return to school without armbands.

Three students, John and Mary Beth Tinker and Christopher Eckhardt, who were made aware of the policy, nonetheless wore armbands to school and were suspended. Of course, students brought action against the school board, and involved school administrators as the result of the suspension.

---

7. Keyishian v. Board of Regents, 385 U.S., p. 603.

Decision

Associate Justice Abe Fortas writing for the majority, in a 7-2 decision, insisted that school regulations promulgated by the school principal prohibiting wearing black armbands as administered under the circumstances "was an unconstitutional denial of students' rights of expression of opinion." [8] Moreover, continued Justice Fortas, there was no reasonable indication that substantial interference with school activities would occur. And, as a matter of fact, there was no disruption of the normal schooling process. What school officials did, maintained Justice Fortas, was "punish petitioners for a silent, passive expression of opinion, unaccompanied by any disorder or disturbance on the part of petitioners." [9] Justice Fortas insisted that "undifferentiated fear or apprehension of disturbance is not enough to overcome the right to freedom of expression." [10]

Discussion

While the issue of censorship of public school library and instructional materials was not directly addressed in this case, the legal principles established are applicable to such cases. The major legal principles established in this decision are as follows:[11]

1. A symbolic act performed to express certain views is a form of free speech which is within the protection of the First Amendment.

2. Pure speech is protected under the Constitution and may not be suppressed by school authorities.

---

8. Tinker v. Des Moines Independent Community School Dist., 393 U.S., p. 503.

9. *Ibid.*, p. 508.

10. *Ibid.*

11. *Ibid.*, p. 503.

3. Teachers and students possess First Amendment rights of freedom of speech and expression even when applied in light of the special environment of schools.

4. "Neither students nor teachers shed their constitutional rights to freedom of speech or expression at the schoolhouse gate." [12]

5. School and state authorities have power to define and control conduct in the schools as long as it is consistent with fundamental constitutional safeguards.

6. "[U]ndifferentiated fear or apprehension of disturbance is not enough to overcome the right to freedom of expression," maintained Justice Fortas.[13] Recognizing that any departure from the norm might cause some disturbance and/or fear Justice Fortas insisted "our Constitution says we must take this risk." [14] The strength, vigor and independence of American democracy is predicated on "this kind of openness." [15] Material and substantial disruption must be shown before free expression can be prohibited.

7. Finally, Justice Fortas issued a philosophical—legal reminder to school boards, and for purposes of this manuscript school boards who might be contemplating some form of censorship that:

> [S]tate-operated schools may not be enclaves of totalitarianism. School officials do not possess absolute authority over their students. [S]tudents may not be regarded as closed-circuit recipients of only that which the State chooses to communicate.[16]

---

12. *Ibid.*
13. *Ibid.*, p. 508.
14. *Ibid.*
15. *Ibid.*
16. *Ibid.*, p. 511.

Keefe v. Geanakos

305 F. Supp. 1091 (D. Mass. 1969),
rev'd and remanded, 418 F.2d
359 (1st Cir. 1969)

Facts

In September 1969 a tenured English teacher in the public schools of Ipswich, Massachusetts, assigned an article in *Atlantic Monthly* to his senior English class. The teacher discussed the article with his class and explained the origin and context of an offensive word contained in the article. Furthermore, the teacher explained the author's reason for including the offensive word in the article and told the students that anyone finding the assignment distasteful could receive an alternative one. Shortly after the assignment was made parents began to complain. The school committee convened a meeting with the teacher present. The teacher was asked if he would agree not to use the article again. The teacher replied that in good conscience he could not so agree. The teacher was suspended, and it was proposed that he be discharged. The teacher had nine years experience and had administrative duties as chairman of the English department. Thus, his teaching duties were somewhat limited. A school committee hearing was scheduled to discuss his dismissal. The teacher sought to enjoin the hearing as a violation of his civil rights. The school committee hearing was not held. The teacher maintained that:

1. As a matter of law his conduct did not warrant discipline; therefore, there were no grounds for a hearing.
2. His conduct was within one's professional competence as a teacher, as a matter of academic freedom, whether the defendants approved or not.
3. He had not been given adequate prior warning by regulations currently in force. An ex post facto ruling in the matter would oppose academic freedom.

147

Decision

The First Circuit Appeals Court with Chief Justice Aldrich writing the opinion reversed the district court decision denying interlocutory injunction. The case was remanded to the United States District Court, District of Massachusetts, for proceedings consistent with the following:

1. The court read the article in question and found that in its entirety it was a valuable discussion of "dissent, protest, radicalism and revolt." [17]

2. The article was in no sense pornographic. Offensiveness of language depends on circumstances, although obscenity standards for adults and students are not "lacking in discrimination or resistance." [18]

3. Furthermore, maintained Justice Aldrich, academic freedom grounded in the First Amendment is basic to a democratic society and merits judicial protection.

Discussion

Academic freedom of teachers was certainly reinforced with this decision. The teacher's educational purpose in discussing the material was not challenged by the court.

Moreover, in determining the appropriate standard, the students themselves, as well as their exposure to similar language outside of the classroom, seemed to be considered. Whether the materials would be considered obscene by community standards apparently did not enter into the court's decision. The court did acknowledge the difference in standards for adults and minors but determined that high school seniors had enough maturity not to be harmed by the

---

17. Keefe v. Geanakos, 418 F.2d, p. 361.
18. *Ibid.*, p. 362.

article. This decision seems consistent with *Tinker*.[19] Under the circumstances students were elevated to an educational level commensurate with their ability to cope with mature concepts.

Parducci v. Rutland

316 F. Supp. 352 (M.D. Ala. 1970)

Facts

A first-year English teacher Marilyn Parducci brought action against members of the school administration and school board of Montgomery County, Alabama because of dismissal for assigning a short story, Kurt Vonnegut's *Welcome to the Monkey House,* to her high school junior class. Of course, parents of some of the students complained. Miss Parducci's teaching ability was never the issue. The principal insisted that she would have received a favorable evaluation except for the single incident. After reading the story the principal and associate superintendent described it as "literary garbage."

Miss Parducci asserted that dismissal for assigning the story violated her First Amendment right to academic freedom. She sought reinstatement to her teaching position.

Decision

Chief Justice Johnson writing the court's opinion insisted that teachers are entitled to First Amendment protection, and that such constitutional security is unaffected by the presence or absence of tenure. Substantial and/or material disruption of the schooling process must be demonstrated in order to restrict teacher First Amendment rights. School officials did not establish that use of the short story caused disruption. Moreover, school officials failed to establish that

---

19. Tinker v. Des Moines Indep. Community School Dist., 393 U.S. 503, 89 S. Ct. 733, 21 L. Ed. 2d 731 (1969).

149

the assignment was inappropriate for the students. This particular short story had not previously been prohibited from classroom use; therefore, the teacher could not be punished for conduct not proscribed in clear and precise terms.

Justice Johnson insisted:

1. Plaintiff should be reinstated for the duration of the contract, with all the rights and privileges held prior to the illegal suspension.
2. Salary should be paid to the plaintiff for both the period during suspension and the remainder of the contract.
3. Defendants must expunge from plaintiff's employment record any reference to suspension and dismissal.
4. Defendants must pay all court costs.

Discussion

In this case the court decisively supported the right of academic freedom for teachers. Moreover, Justice Johnson asserted that presence or absence of tenure under state law does not affect constitutional rights.

The state's interest in protecting students from inappropriate reading materials was balanced against the teacher's academic freedom. Justice Johnson determined the short story was not obscene and was indeed appropriate reading for juniors in high school. In making this decision the court relied on its own judgement indicating the literary and social value of the questioned material. This is in contrast to *Keefe* where the court reviewed and evaluated the school committee's decision in determining the value of objectional material. Further, the court was not explicit in stating whether the school board's claim that the material was "literary garbage" was arbitrary. Likewise the court did not address the constitutionality of parents' complaints.

A most important question arising from the decision is the matter of future reading assignments. Justice Johnson asserted that a teacher may not be dismissed unless prior notice has been received that assignment of particular material is impermissible. School authorities in this case had tried to obtain agreement from the teacher not to assign the short story in the future. The teacher refused to agree.

This issue raises a provocative question. What if the school board banned the questionable book—simply prohibited by school board policy the book's use. And suppose the teacher ignored the school board policy and assigned the book anyway. We now have a hard case of insubordination. The provocative question is: Would the *Parducci* Court still maintain First Amendment academic freedom for the teacher? If the answer is yes then the *Parducci* Court ultimately has the power to determine the educational value of curricula.

§ 4.2. Students' Rights to Read, Inquire, and Receive Information.

Overview

Extension of constitutional rights to public school students has not been an organized professional movement but has resulted chiefly from case law. The landmark case of *Tinker* has been the principal legal influence in establishing students' rights in public schools. While the issue of censorship of public school library and instructional materials was not directly addressed in *Tinker*,[20] the legal principles established are applicable to such cases. *Tinker's* major legal principles have already been recorded earlier in this chapter. Additional decisions relating to the emerging rights of students to learn, to know, and to receive information in a free marketplace of ideas are presented in *Virginia*

---

20. Tinker v. Des Moines Indep. Community School Dist., 393 U.S. 503, 89 S. Ct. 733, 21 L. Ed. 2d 731 (1969).

State Board of Pharmacy, Minarcini, Right to Read and
Pratt v. Pico.

Virginia State Board of Pharmacy v. Virginia Citizens Consumer Council, Inc.

425 U.S. 748, 96 S. Ct. 1817,
48 L. Ed. 2d 346 (1976)

Facts

A Virginia statute [21] declared that it was unprofessional
conduct for a licensed pharmacist to advertise prices of prescription drugs. A citizen suffering from chronic illnesses
which required her to take prescription drugs daily, the
Virginia Citizen's Consumer Council, Inc., and the Virginia
State American Federation of Labor and Congress of Industrial Organizations challenged the validity of the statute
under both First and Fourteenth Amendments of the
United States Constitution.

Decision

The District Court [22] had declared the statute void and
enjoined the Virginia State Board of Pharmacy from
enforcing the regulation. On appeal the United States
Supreme Court with Associate Justice Blackmun writing
the majority opinion sustained the District Court's decision.

Discussion

This case is pertinent in any discussion with respect to
censoring school library and instructional materials since it

---

21. Va. Code Ann. § 54-524.35 (1974).

22. Virginia State Board of Pharmacy v. Virginia Consumers Council,
Inc., 373 F. Supp. 683 (E.D. Va. 1974).

has been cited as an important precedent in subsequent censorship cases. The right to receive information is the central issue in the decision.

The following is the judicial logic of *Virginia Pharmacy* applicable to a school censorship case:

1. First Amendment protection is enjoyed by recipients of information and not solely by those who seek to disseminate the information.[23]
2. Freedom of speech presupposes a willing speaker; where a speaker exists, the constitutional protection envelops the communication, for both source and recipients.[24]

Of course *Virginia Pharmacy* concerned rights of adults. There is always the nagging constitutional question concerning adults' rights as compared with students. The *Minarcini* court did not differentiate between the rights of minors and adult rights. The *Ginsberg*[25] Court did find a difference. The *Tinker*[26] decision is an expansive and inclusive homily with potentially far reaching implications concerning First Amendment student rights in censorship cases.

Virginia Pharmacy[27] recognized that free speech "presupposes a willing speaker." The *Minarcini* court never

---

23. Virginia State Board of Pharmacy v. Virginia Citizens Consumer Council, Inc., 425 U.S. 748, 757 (1976).

23. *Ibid.,* p. 756.

24. *Ibid.,* p. 756.

25. Ginsberg v. New York, 390 U.S. 629, 88 S. Ct. 1274, 20 L. Ed. 2d 195 (1968).

26. Tinker v. Des Moines Indep. Community School Dist., supra note 20.

27. Virginia State Board of Pharmacy v. Virginia Consumers Council, Inc., supra note 24.

really identified the willing speaker.[28] The *Salvail*[29] court also indirectly relied on *Virginia Pharmacy*. The point made was that the Supreme Court decision in *Virginia Pharmacy* has been of limited influence in elementary and secondary censorship cases; yet, the thread is present.

Minarcini v. Strongsville City School District

384 F. Supp. 698 (N.D. Ohio 1974), *aff'd in part,
rev'd in part,* 541 F.2d 577 (6th Cir. 1976)

Facts

The parents of five high school students brought action, on behalf of their children, against the Strongsville, Ohio City School District, the school board, and the superintendent. The central issue is that the school board refused to accept the faculty's recommendation to purchase particular novels for use in the English curriculum and in addition removed particular books from the school library.

Plaintiffs claimed constitutional violation for obvious reasons—certain novels had been disapproved for classroom use and others had been withdrawn from the school library.

Decision

The District Court with Justice Kanpansky writing the opinion found no constitutional violation. On appeal the Sixth Circuit Court of Appeals with Justice Edwards writing the opinion separated the complaint into two issues:

---

28. Minarcini v. Strongsville City School Dist., 384 F. Supp. 698 (N.D. Ohio 1974); William A. Eagles, "Constitutional Law—Right of Public School Children to Receive Information—Minarcini v. Strongsville City School District," *Wake Forest Law Review* 13 (1977): 834-41.

29. Salvail v. Nashua Bd. of Educ., 469 F. Supp. 1269, (D.N.H. 1979).

(1) the selection and removal of textbooks; and (2) the removal of library books. The Circuit Court affirmed the District Court's decision upholding the school board's authority to select and remove textbooks. However, Justice Edwards maintained that neither the state and/or school board is required to establish libraries in schools. Once established a library becomes a privilege that cannot be withdrawn because of political or social tastes of the school board. Justice Edwards further insisted that library books can be removed only for constitutionally allowable reasons. Finally, Justice Edwards determined that library books withdrawal violated students' First Amendment rights to receive information — "the removal of books from a school library is a much more serious burden upon freedom of classroom discussion than the action found unconstitutional in *Tinker.*" [30] On appeal the Supreme Court refused to review the case.

Discussion

A significant factor about this decision is the unquestionable extension of First Amendment rights to school children. The decision rejected the indoctrination concept of education in which schools exist *in loco parentis.* Instead, Justice Edwards supported students' rights within the philosophical context that the school is a "marketplace of ideas." Justice Edwards asserted that removal of library books violated students' constitutional right to know and receive information. Yet, in a contrasting response, Justice Edwards contended that school board action did not significantly hamper teachers' expression.

The *Minarcini* court did not establish judicial guidelines concerning the equality of rights of children and adults in receiving information. Yet, in jurisdictions where this case

---

30. Minarcini v. Strongsville City School Dist., 541 F.2d p. 584.

has been accepted precedent, students' rights have been elevated equal to those of adults.

Right to Read Defense Committee of Chelsea v. School Committee of Chelsea

454 F. Supp. 703 (D. Mass. 1978)

Facts

The Chelsea, Massachusetts school committee removed an anthology entitled *Male and Female* from the high school library. The school committee action was prompted by a parent's objection to a single poem selection in the book, *The City to a Young Girl,* written by a high school student from New York City. After reading the poem the Chelsea School Committee determined the poem was "filthy" and "offensive." [31] The school principal, also reading the poem, decided to remove the poem from the book and keep both poem and book in his office. The full text of the questioned poem written by Jody Caravaglia is as follows:

The City to a Young Girl

The city is
One million horney lip-smacking men
Screaming for my body
The streets are long conveyor belts
Loaded with suckling pigs
All begging for
a lay
a little pussy

---

31. Right to Read Defense Committee of Chelsea v. School Committee of Chelsea, 454 F. Supp. 707.

a bit of tit
a leg to rub against
a handful of ass
the connoisseurs of cunt
Every day, every night
Pressing in on me closer and closer,
I swat them off like flies
but they keep coming back,
I'm a good piece of meat.

Plaintiffs in this case were the Right to Read Committee, which included parents, students, teachers, and a librarian. The plaintiffs sought a restraining order requiring the book to be returned to the library intact. Plaintiffs insisted that removal of the book violated First Amendment rights of students, faculty, and library staff.

The school committee responded by claiming complete authority to remove books from the library. Moreover, the school committee insisted they were not required to purchase the book; therefore, the school committee concluded the book could be removed at their discretion.

Decision

The district court with Justice Tauro writing the opinion determined that removal of the book infringed on First Amendment rights of the students and faculty of Chelsea High School. Justice Tauro insisted:

[A] school should be a readily accessible warehouse of ideas ... the First Amendment is not merely a mantle which students and faculty must doff when they take their places in the classroom.[32]

Justice Tauro maintained that the "student who discovers the magic of the library is on the way to a life-long

---

32. *Ibid.*

experience of self-education and enrichment." [33] Exposure to a variety of ideas and philosophies is not dangerous continued Justice Tauro "the danger is in mind control." [34]

Finally, Justice Tauro ordered the book returned intact to the library. The school committee was ordered to pay plaintiffs' legal fees.

Discussion

Justice Tauro identified the underlying conflict as tension between the school committee's necessary administrative and policy discretion authority colliding with the First Amendment rights of students and teachers in the school system. Once again Justice Tauro reaffirmed that local school boards are the policy makers for public education and have complete authority to select books. Yet, their discretion, in the area of book selection and removal, maintained Justice Tauro, does not envelop the school library if such book removal violates the First Amendment rights of others.

Justice Tauro took issue with the school committee's reliance on *Presidents Council* [35] for legal defense: That decision, insisted Justice Tauro, was inappropriate because the book did not meet the standards of irrelevancy, obsolescence, or obscenity as defined in *Presidents Council.* Moreover, there was no substantial governmental interest demonstrated, justifying removal of the book.

It should be pointed out that this case came out of a federal district court located in the First Circuit Court of Appeals jurisdiction. The decision follows the trend established in the First Circuit.

---

33. *Ibid.*, p. 715.
34. *Ibid.*
35. Presidents Council, Dist. 25 v. Community School Bd. No. 25, 457 F.2d 289 (2d Cir.), *cert. denied,* 409 U.S. 998 (1972).

Pratt v. Independent School District No. 831, Forest Lake, Minnesota

670 F.2d 771 (8th Cir. 1982)

Facts

In 1977 several parents of high school children became concerned about the use of "The Lottery" and a "trailer" film in American literature courses. "The Lottery" is a short story by Shirley Jackson and the films were produced by the Encyclopedia Britannica Educational Corporation. In February, 1978 a meeting was held with approximately fifty people attending including school board members and teachers. Both films were shown at the beginning of the meeting. After the viewing, teachers explained reasons for using them and justified precisely the importance of the films to the American literature courses. Shortly after the meeting three parents filed a formal citizens request that the films be removed from the curriculum for the following reasons: (1) the " 'theme or purpose' of this was 'the breakdown of family values and traditions' "; (2) the films may cause children to question " 'their own family loyalities' "; and (3) the films realism " 'accentuates its brutality and senselessness in our times.' " [36]

In late March another meeting was scheduled (the people who attended the meeting were named the Committee for Challenged Materials) and once again approximately fifty people attended, and once again the films were viewed and teachers promulgated reasons for using the films. And again those people opposing the films raised the same questions aired at the February meeting. At the conclusion of the meeting the Challenge Committee made the following recommendations: (1) the films be discontinued at the

---

36. Pratt v. Independent School Dist. No. 831, 670 F.2d, p. 774.

Junior High School; and (2) that the films be included in the senior high school curriculum but before showing the films, an information sheet be distributed among the students' parents advising them that they could exclude their children from viewing the films.[37]

The Challenge Committee recommendations were appealed to the school board and the school board voted four to three rejecting a motion to "... 'accept and confirm' ... the recommendations."[38] The school board then voted four to three to delete entirely the films from the curriculum. The plaintiffs — students and parents — began the litigious process. The federal district court of Minnesota with Justice Miles W. Lord writing the opinion, ordered "the films be reinstated to their prior place in the curriculum."[39] Yet, Justice Lord provided the school board with an opportunity to explain and justify the board's action when viewed against the First Amendment. The school board though, rather than present additional evidence, submitted the following resolution:

> The motion picture version of "The Lottery" and the trailer film discussing the short story graphically place an exaggerated and undue emphasis on violence and bloodshed which is not appropriate or suitable for showing in a high school classroom and which has the effect of distorting the short story and overshadowing its many otherwise valuable and educationally important themes.[40]

Justice Lord rejected the resolution and insisted the resolution did not "constitute 'cognizable, credible, evidence as to any legitimate reason for excluding' the films from the

---

37. *Ibid.*
38. *Ibid.*
39. *Ibid.*, p. 775.
40. *Ibid.*

curriculum." [41] The school board appealed to the Eighth Circuit Court of Appeals.

Decision

On appeal the Eighth Circuit Court of Appeals, with Justice Heaney writing the opinion, affirmed the lower court's decision and insisted that: (1) school board decision was predicated on "ideological and religious" reasons and not because the films distorted the short story and contained violent scenes; and (2) the school board decision had placed restriction on protected speech with an unjustified assumption that the printed book which remained available in the library satisfied free speech requirements. [42] Thus, the school board decision violated students' First Amendment free speech rights.

Discussion

Once again we have the classic confrontation between a school board predicating policy on personal ideological and/or religious viewpoints and in this case students and parents who are agitated enough to seek a resolution to the confrontation. Justice Heaney acknowledged that school boards are the policy makers for public schools and appropriately those policies "may properly reflect local community views and values as to educational content and methodology." [43]

However, maintained Justice Heaney, "school boards do not have absolute right to remove materials from the curriculum." [44] Justice Heaney then proceeded to run the

---

41. *Ibid.*
42. *Ibid.*, pp. 776-78.
43. *Ibid.*, p. 775.
44. *Ibid.*, p. 776.

most recent judicial history with respect to censorship and insisted that school board's discretion could best be cast in the framework as policy making intuitively mandated from an ideological and/or religious viewpoint. With the ideological and/or religious framework for the purpose of judicial analysis established, Justice Heaney proceeded to examine the school board's position.

The school board's major contention, and one parenthetically that was filed after the district court provided the school board with an opportunity to file reasons justifying its action, was that the films "The Lottery" and the trailer film placed an exaggerated "emphasis on violence and bloodshed ... which has the effect of distorting the short story." [45] Justice Heaney maintained that the school board description "is simply not supported by the facts." [46] There was only a single scene depicting physical violence in the entire two films. Moreover, suggested Justice Heaney, that scene "is faithfully adapted from the short story." [47]

In responding to the school board's position that the book version, was still located in the library and remained available to teachers and students, Justice Heaney said:

> The board seeks to justify its action by pointing out that the short story remains available to teachers and students in the library in printed form and a photographic recording. This fact is not decisive. Restraint on protected speech generally cannot be justified by the fact that there may be other times, places or circumstances for such expression. The symbolic effect of removing the films from the curriculum is more significant than the resulting limitation of access to the story. The board has used its official power to perform an act clearly indicating that the ideas con-

---

45. *Ibid.*, p. 778.
46. *Ibid.*
47. *Ibid.*

tained in the films are unacceptable and should not be discussed or considered. This message is not lost on students and teachers, and its chilling effect is obvious.[48]

The facts are so clearly and plainly presented, suggested Justice Heaney. The school board policy satisfied no compelling state interest and the policy effect existed "for interfering with the students' right to receive information."[49]

Finally, said Justice Heaney, even though judicial authority over school boards is limited, the judiciary has "an obligation to uphold the Constitution to protect the fundamental rights of all citizens."[50]

Justice Heaney's concluding statement is an imperative reminder to school administration and school board members:

"The Lottery" is not a comforting film. But there is more at issue here than the sensibilities of those viewing the films. What is at stake is the right to receive information and to be exposed to controversial ideas—a fundamental First Amendment right. If these films can be banned by those opposed to their ideological theme, then a precedent is set for the removal of any such work.[51]

---

48. *Ibid.*, p. 779.
49. *Ibid.*
50. *Ibid.*
51. *Ibid.*

Pico v. Board of Education, Island Tree Union Free School District No. 26

638 F.2d 404 (2d Cir. 1980)

(Rehearing and Rehearing En Banc Denied March 3, 1981)

Facts

This case was brought on appeal from the federal district court (Eastern District, New York) seeking declaratory and injunctive relief from school board actions removing nine books from the school library and curriculum. The nine books included three non-fiction, four autobiographies, two anthologies, and one non-fiction.[52] The federal district court, with Judge George C. Pratt writing the decision, had dismissed the class action complaint. Plaintiffs appealed to the Second Circuit Appeals Court.

Decision

Justice Sifton suggested that school board members "acted because of political motivation and whether books were removed because of their ideas precluding summary judgement."[53] Thus, the Second Circuit Appeals Court reversed and remanded for trial on the above issues. But, alas, the school board was not about to travel that route. The board appealed to the United States Supreme Court and on October 12, 1981, the Court agreed to hear the case.

---

52. The books are: (1) Eldridge Cleaver, *Soul on Ice;* Alice Childress, *A Hero Ain't Nothing But a Sandwich;* Bernard Malamud, *The Fixer; Go Ask Alice,* Anonymous; Kurt Vonnegut, Jr., *Slaughterhouse Five;* Langston Hughes (ed.), *The Best Short Stories by Negro Writers;* Richard Wright, *Black Boy;* Oliver La Farge, *Laughing Boy;* Desmond Morris, *The Naked Ape;* Jerome Archer (ed.), *A Reader for Writers.*

53. Pico v. Board of Educ., 638 F.2d, p. 404.

It should be noted that the *Pico* Court was split 2-1;—Justices Sifton and Newman voting the majority and Justice Mansfield writing a dissenting opinion.

Discussion

Indeed, what are the circumstances that seem to circumvent the well established practice of the Second Circuit Appeals Court supporting school boards in censorship activities? Justice Sifton reviewed in absolute detail the questionable publications and juxtaposed the constitutional questions against the Second Circuit Appeals Court recent elementary and secondary censorship case history. But more importantly Justice Sifton juxtaposed school board political and religious activities against constitutional questions. What emerges from Justice Sifton's positions is, what the school board did—political and religious motivation and views—spoke so convincingly that their constitutional justification were all but silent—the extent of political and religious motivation mooted explanatory intent.

The record is very clear. School board members attended a conference sponsored by the People of New York United—supposedly a conservation organization composed of parents concerned about the organizations and governance of education.[54] A part of the conference focused on textbooks and library books control and of course produced an objectionable book list. The school board returned home and in time some members began examining the high school library catalog cards determining which of the objectionable books were in the high school library. One evening, in early November 1975, two school board members, while attending a "Winter School Night," asked the custodian to

---

54. Speakers at the Conference were from Heritage Foundation, Washington, D.C.; Arizona; and Kanawa County, West Virginia.

let them in the school library. While plowing through the card catalog searching for books on their list, they were surprised by the school principal. The board members explained somewhat what they were doing.

More weeks elapsed and at the conclusion of the February 1976 school board meeting the high school principals were asked to stay. A lengthy discussion followed and the high school principals and junior high principals were asked to remove the books from the library shelves. Three days later the school superintendent protested the banning action:

> My objection to direct action banning all the books ... is that we don't know who developed the list, nor the criteria they used. I don't believe we should accept and act on someone else's list, unless we first study the books ourselves. ... We already have a policy ... designed expressly to handle such problems. ... Unilateral banning by the Board, without input from the staff, would surely create a furious uproar. ... I don't believe you want such an uproar, and I certainly don't.[55]

The school board rejected the school superintendent's recommendations and again directed that all copies of the library books in question be removed. The public response was shortly underway. The school board responded in a manner that is often characterized as "school board mentality"—instead of coming to grips with the issue, discredit the opposition. And that is just what the school board did. The school board suggested that the Teacher Union leaders were simply "attempting to discredit the Board and win the seats for two union-backed lackeys." [56]

The conflict intensified. The school board devoted the entire March issue of the *Newsletter* to its position — "lies

---

55. Pico v. Board of Educ., 638 F.2d., p. 409.
56. *Ibid.*

and misinformation which has been spread by the teachers union . . . fighting to keep books in our schools which are offensive to Christians, Jews, Blacks, and all Americans in general." [57]

In a late March public meeting the school superintendent again protested school board censorship and reminded the board that the union's contract provided that teachers had the right to "introduce and explore controversial material . . . appropriate to grade level." [58] Again the school superintendent urged that books be returned to the school libraries. The school board refused the request. However, in early April the school superintendent and the school board jointly agreed on a book review committee. Throughout April, May, and June the book review committee met on five different occasions and voted to return all books except three to the library shelves.[59] On July 18, 1976, the school board, in public meeting, rejected the book review committee's recommendations, with two exceptions — voting on each book separately — and directed that all other books be removed from the school libraries and curriculum instruction program.[60]

Finally, one other event must be recorded. In the middle of the book banning fomentation (May, 1976) there was a school board election. Two of the incumbents ran successfully and there is every reason to believe that the book banning issue re-elected the incumbent members.

Of course litigation followed school board censorship—January 1977. The school board countered with:

---

57. *Ibid.*, p. 410.

58. *Ibid.*, p. 411.

59. The three books not returned were: Desmond Morris' *The Naked Ape*; Piri Thomas' *Down These Mean Streets*; and Eldridge Cleaver's *Soul on Ice*.

60. The two books which the school board voted to return were Oliver La Farge's *Laughing Boy*; and Richard Wright's *Black Boy*.

167

(1) a press release defending the board's action; and (2) a survey of school district parents' attitudes toward school board action.[61]

In early August 1979 Judge Pratt relying on *President's Council* found for the school board. Thus, Justice Sifton now occupied center stage writing the Second Circuit Court of Appeals majority opinion.

Justice Sifton began by recognizing the enormous First Amendment complexities applicable to secondary school children. Justice Sifton examined the major landmark decisions that are now familiar in this manuscript—*Tinker, Barnett, Epperson, Pacifica Foundation, Ginsberg, Keyishian, Gobitis,* and the list is extensive.

Next, Justice Sifton acknowledged that courts should not interfere with conflicts that occur with the day to day school operation. Yet, something unusual had happened, maintained Justice Sifton:

> What we have instead is an unusual and irregular intervention in the school libraries' operation . . . this intervention has occurred under circumstances, including the explanations for their actions . . . which so far from clarifying the scope and intentions behind the official action, create instead grave questions concerning both subjects.[62]

Continuing Justice Sifton insisted that school board "irregular and ambiguous activities created a " *prima facie* case" which necessitated judicial intervention:

> . . . because of the real threat that the school officials' irregular and ambiguous handling of the issue will, even despite the best intentions, create

---

61. Judge Sifton questioned the school board legal counsel's "propriety" in mailing the questionnaire but attorney defended on reason that the suit was class action.

62. Pico v. Board of Educ., supra note 53, p. 414.

misunderstanding as to the scope of their activities which will serve to suppress freedom of expression.[63]

Judge Sifton insisted that the school board was insensitive to First Amendment issues. Moreover, the school board never provided any forum and/or leadership for a reasonable and open debate concerning books "that are 'anti-Christian' or 'anti-American.' " [64] It seemed, said Justice Sifton, that school board members were less concerned with sanitizing the libraries than in expressing "an official policy with regard to God and country of uncertain and indefinite content which is to be ignored by pupils, librarians, and teachers at their peril." [65]

So the sum totality of school board activities, irrespective of school superintendent advice, was "in a manner calculated to create public uproar" and with the book banning " 'most of the parents . . . will back us to the hilt' " and the guarantee of majority support is omnipresent.[66] School board activity with majority support would appear to satisfy the state compelling interest in education and First Amendment free speech. But school board argument is too simplistic in this case at bar.

On the contrary, said Justice Sifton, school board political and religious convolutions created an atmosphere that was more feared than the policy itself:

> [T]he erratic, unfair and arbitrary administration of policy with regard to speech in schools is as much to be feared as the contents of the policy itself as a source of First Amendment violations.[67]

---

63. *Ibid.*, p. 415.
64. *Ibid.*, p. 416.
65. *Ibid.*
66. *Ibid.*
67. *Ibid.*, p. 417.

Finally, Justice Sifton, in dismissing school board's remaining assertion—the school board had suggested that was "substantial and material" for its activities and that all decisions were "possessed of sufficient, procedural regularity" — insisted that such pleadings "were simply pretexts for the suppression of free speech." [68] The school board, maintained Justice Sifton, really never had children's interest at hand but were interested in "establishing those views as the correct and orthodox ones for all purposes in the particular community." [69] Thus, said Justice Sifton this case fails First Amendment free speech muster on the following: (1) the children's welfare and education were never the real issues for book removal; (2) the school board's reasons for book removal were "confusion" and "incoherence"; (3) school board's informal and dilatory manner and method of procedure; (4) the *ex post facto* appointment of a book review committee and then ignoring the committee's recommendations; (5) strong professional opposition; and (6) "substantive irregularities ... of reviewing works by such generally recognized authors as Swift, the late Richard Wright, and Bernard Malamud, whose book, *The Fixer,* was, indeed, an assigned high school reading text.[70] As already indicated the Supreme Court on October 12, 1982, agreed to hear the school board's appeal.

Board of Education, Island Tree Union Free School District No. 26 v. Pico

Case No. 80-2043, 50 L.W. 4831 (1982)

Decision

On June 25, 1982, the Supreme Court (in a five-four decision—Justices Marshall, Stevens, Blackmun, and White

---

68. *Ibid.*
69. *Ibid.*
70. *Ibid.*, p. 418.

joined the majority judgement) with Justice Brennan
writing the majority opinion affirmed the Second Circuit
Court of Appeals decision.

Discussion

Justice Brennan spent little time detailing the facts
already spelled out in considerable detail by the lower
court's review. Yet, Justice Brennan acknowledged the limited issue before the Court. This case, maintained Justice
Brennan, involved no curriculum issues, no textbook or any
other books with assigned readings, and no classroom intrusion. The constitutional questions did not involve the acquisition of books — "We emphasize at the outset the limited
nature of the substantive question presented by the case
before us." [71] Thus, acknowledged Justice Brennan, the
only issues "in this case are library books" and "the suppression of ideas." [72] Moreover, the issue both substantively and procedurally raises only two questions, maintained Justice Brennan. Question one: Does the First
Amendment "impose any limitations" on school board's
discretion to remove book from the library? Question Two:
If the answer to question one is yes then does the evidence
indicate that the school board "exceeded those limitations?" [73]

With the appropriate issues delineated, Justice Brennan
proceeded with the response. A brief review of major
Supreme Court decisions concerning students' rights was
presented—*Meyer, Pierce, Epperson, Tinker, Barnette,* and
Keyishian to mention just a few. Justice Brennan suggested
that these precedents focused " 'not only on the role of the
First Amendment in fostering individual self-expression

---

71. Board of Educ. v. Pico, 50 L. W., p. 4833.

72. *Ibid.*, pp. 4834-36.

73. *Ibid.*

but also on its role in affording the public access to discussion, debate, and the dissemination of information and ideas.' " [74] Moreover, suggested Justice Brennan, the Court has on many occasions insisted that the " 'Constitution protects the right to receive information and ideas.' " [75] The right to receive information is derived from free speech and press and encapsulates First Amendment rights for the "sender" to distribute literature and the right to receive such literature. Logically, continues Justice Brennan's homily, the disseminations of information and ideas mean nothing if there is no one to receive them. Thus, a school library establishes an environment where the "sender" and "receiver" juxtaposed under First Amendment free speech and press. Moreover, insisted Justice Brennan, "the right to receive ideas is a necessary predicate to the *recipient's* meaningful exercise of his own rights of speech, press, and political freedom." [76] School children not only have the right to First Amendment self-expression but also First Amendment right to receive information and ideas. But yet, Justice Brennan acknowledged that all First Amendment student rights "must be construed 'in light of the special characteristic of the school environment.' " [77] So, student First Amendment rights are conditional.

With the historical review completed and judicial philosophical underpinning established, Justice Brennan proceeds to answer the first question. The special characteristics, insisted Justice Brennan, "of the school make that environment especially appropriate for the recognition

---

74. *Ibid.*, p. 4835.

75. *Ibid.*

76. *Ibid.* See also Martin v. Struthers, 318 U.S. 141, 143 (1943) and Lamont v. Postmaster General, 381 U.S. 301, 308 (1965) for a more detailed treatment of First Amendment "sender-receiver" concept.

77. *Ibid.*

of the First Amendment rights of students." [78] Justice Brennan described the school library as "a place dedicated to 'knowledge,' 'quiet,' 'beauty' . . . is the principal locus of . . . freedom," and a place where students voluntarily participate in self-education. [79]

The school board has relied on the basic supposition that they had absolute "unfettered discretion to 'transmit community values'" throughout the school system. [80] Justice Brennan suggested that school board claim might be applicable to compulsory curriculum matters in the classroom but "misplaced where" as in the school library "voluntary inquiry . . . holds sway." [81] Yes, acknowledged Justice Brennan, school boards do have a "substantial legitimate role to play in the determination of the school library content"; however, "that discretion may not be exercised in a narrow partisan or political manner." [82] Justice Brennan once again affirmed that "Our Constitution does not permit the official suppression of ideas" and/or encourage "officially prescribed orthodoxy." [83]

Thus insisted Justice Brennan:

> [W]e hold that local school boards may not remove books from school library shelves simply because they dislike the ideas contained in those books and seek by their removal to "prescribe what shall be orthodox in politics, nationalism, religion, or other matters of opinion." [84]

With the answer to the first question fundamentally established, Justice Brennan proceeded to the next

---

78. *Ibid.*
79. *Ibid.*, pp. 4835-36.
80. *Ibid.*
81. *Ibid.*
82. *Ibid.*
83. *Ibid.*
84. *Ibid.*

question concerning evidentiary materials before the District Court. "We conclude that the materials do raise such a question" insisted Justice Brennan.[85] First, the school board had no "established regular and facially unbiased procedure for the review of controversial materials." [86] Second, the school board ignored the advice of the professional staff. Third, that while school board initially defended their action on grounds that the books contained " 'obscenities, blasphemies, and perversion beyond description,' " one removed book contained no such language.[87] Fourth, books singled out were on the PONYU hit list and as such the school board never conducted an independent review of library books. Thus, concluded Justice Brennan, "petitioners removal procedures were highly irregular and ad hoc—the antithesis of those procedures that might tend to allay suspicions regarding petitioners motivations." [88]

Justice Blackmun concurring in the judgement and concurring in part presented a somewhat different First Amendment perspective. Justice Blackmun rejected the notion that school libraries and the right to receive information was the constitutional centerpiece in this case at bar. Instead, Justice Blackmun "suggested that certain forms of state discrimination *between* ideas are improper." [89] Justice Blackmun describes the issue as striking the proper balance between state authority "to regulate education" and First Amendment constitutional restriction.[90] As such, insisted Justice Blackmun, "we must reconcile the schools' 'inculcative' function with the First Amendment bar on

---

85. *Ibid.*
86. *Ibid.*, p. 4837.
87. *Ibid.* (The book referred to is *A Reader for Writers.*)
88. *Ibid.*
89. *Ibid.*, p. 4838.
90. *Ibid.*

'prescription of orthodoxy.' " [91] And in Justice Blackmun's view that proper balance is achieved as such:

> [T]hat school officials may not remove books for the *purpose* of restricting access to the political ideas or social perspectives discussed in them, when that action is motivated simply by the officials' disapproval of the ideas involved.[92]

Justice White, while concurring in the judgement, saw no "necessity at this point for discussing the extent to which the First Amendment limits the school board's discretion to remove books from the school libraries." [93]

Chief Justice Burger, with whom Justices Powell, Rehnquist, and O'Connor join, wrote a biting dissenting opinion. Justice Burger proceeded issue by issue rebuting Justice Brennan's position and insisted that school boards not federal judges should make decisions concerning library book selection.[94] Ultimately, insisted Justice Burger, "the federal courts will be the judge of whether the motivation for book removal was 'valid' or reasonable." [95] Yet, maintained Justice Burger, "local control of education involved democracy in a microcosm." [96] School boards are elected by the people and are subject to parent influence and often control and as such are accountable for board actions. What you have, insisted Justice Burger, is the necessary check on school board's discretion by the constituency who could remove them from office in the next election. And finally, suggested Justice Burger, even if parents and students are unsuccessful in convincing the school board of the

---

91. *Ibid.*
92. *Ibid.*
93. *Ibid.*, p. 4832.
94. *Ibid.*, p. 4840.
95. *Ibid.*, p. 4841.
96. *Ibid.*

175

inappropriateness of book removal, "they have alternative sources. . . . Books may be acquired from book stores, public libraries, or other alternative sources." [97]

So the Supreme Court is divided on public school censorship issues. But the *Pico* majority decision is a much stronger opinion than first blush indicates. Four justices in the *Pico* majority worry about school board policy predicated on personal political and religious ideological preferences. Justice White, the other member of the *Pico* majority, was concerned at least to the extent "I am not inclined to disagree with the Court of Appeals on such a fact-bound issue." [98] However, and in reality, Justice White has deferred his opinion until another day "When the findings of fact and conclusions of law are made by the District Court." [99] The four justices in the *Pico* minority would allow greater latitude for school boards in library material selection and removal. Such reasoning is grounded in the "local mores and views of the community" predilection — "elected officials express the views of their community." [100] So the judicial philosophy for both majority and minority is established. And, perhaps, Justice White will determine the Court's majority identity in future censorship cases. Justice Burger is surely right on one issue but perhaps for the wrong reason — "Ultimately, the federal courts will be the judge of whether the motivation for book removal was 'valid' or 'reasonable'." [101]

---

97. *Ibid.*, p. 4842.
98. *Ibid.*, p. 4839.
99. *Ibid.*
100. *Ibid.*, p. 4840.
101. *Ibid.*, p. 4841.

§ 4.3. Right of School Boards to Select and Remove Library and Instructional Materials.

Overview

School boards are empowered through state constitutional and statutory authority to prescribe curriculum and to select library books and other instructional materials. However, school board authority must always be balanced with the constitutional rights of teachers, students, and parents. Cases presented in this category reveal the courts' line of reasoning as the judiciary has sought to bring about a constitutional school board authority balance when censorship is involved.

Any discussion of the legal concept of school board's authority to select and remove books and instructional materials must begin with the United States Supreme Court's *Meyer* [102] decision. *Meyer's* importance has already been chronicled earlier in this chapter. However, there are two important salient quotes that should be shared again: (1) "the calling of modern language teachers, with the opportunities of pupils to acquire knowledge, and with the power of parents to control the education of their own"; and (2) "but this cannot be coerced by methods which conflict with the Constitution,—a desirable end cannot be promoted by prohibited means." [103]

Also, in this introductory statement, the judicial dictum of the Sixth Circuit Appeals Court in *Minarcini* [104] must always be omnipresent. In ruling against the school board the *Minarcini* court insisted that neither the state and/or school board were required to establish libraries. However,

---

102. Meyer v. Nebraska, 262 U.S. 390, 43 S. Ct. 625, 67 L. Ed. 1042 (1923).

103. *Ibid.*, p. 1046.

104. Minarcini v. Strongsville City School Dist., 541 F.2d 577 (6th Cir. 1976).

once established libraries were a privilege, the *Minarcini* court maintained, that cannot be withdrawn because of the school board political and social tastes—a type of "tenure" for library books.

Presidents Council, District 25 v. Community School Board No. 25

457 F.2d 289 (2d Cir.), *cert. denied,*
409 U.S. 998 (1972)

Facts

On March 31, 1971, Community School Board No. 25, Queens, New York, removed all copies of Piri Thomas' novel *Down These Mean Streets* from all junior high school libraries in the school district. In June of that year the school board passed a unanimous motion retaining the book in school libraries that previously had the book. However, the book was made available to students only on direct loan to their parents. Teachers were allowed to discuss the book in class and assign it for outside reading. The librarian was not penalized.

The Presidents Council, District 25 (Plaintiffs) is an organization of current and past presidents of various parent-teacher groups, three junior high school students, parents and guardians of students, two teachers, a librarian, and a junior high school principal. The appellants maintained that removal of the book violated their First Amendment rights.

Decision

The Second Circuit Court of Appeals with Justice Mulligan writing the opinion acknowledged that the New York legislature delegated authority to select materials in public school libraries to community school boards. Moreover, Justice Mulligan insisted, limited access to the

178

book did not violate the First Amendment. Thus, said Justice Mulligan, it was inappropriate to review the school board's decision.

Discussion

This was the first judicial decision supporting the concept that a school board had the authority to limit access to a specific book which the school board considered inappropriate for students. The Second Circuit Court of Appeals found no First Amendment violation and, therefore, did not consider it necessary to review the decision of the school board. "We do not consider it appropriate for this court to review either the wisdom or efficacy of the determinations of the board." [105] Justice Mulligan likewise acknowledged that administrative procedures available in New York to review school board decisions had not been exhausted. Justice Mulligan made no distinction between the school board's authority to either select and/or remove books. Justice Mulligan also did not allude to the school board's social and/or political tastes.

On appeal the Supreme Court denied certiorari [106] with Justices Potter, Stewart, and William O. Douglas dissenting. In his dissenting opinion Justice Douglas maintained:

> At school the children are allowed to discuss the contents of the book and social problems it portrays. They can do everything but read it. This in my mind lessens somewhat the contention that the subject matter of the book is not proper.[107]

---

105. Presidents Council Dist. 25 v. Community School Bd. No. 25, 457 F.2d, p. 291.

106. Presidents Council Dist. 25 v. Community School Bd. No. 25, 409 U.S. 998 (1972).

107. Presidents Council Dist. 25 v. Community School Bd. No. 25, 409 U.S., p. 999.

Justice Douglas further contended the First Amendment is a preferred right upholding the "right to hear, to learn, to know." [108]

It should be pointed out that at approximately the same time the Second Circuit was deciding *Presidents Council* the Sixth Circuit was deciding *Minarcini* with a decided opposing position insisting that library book removal constituted First Amendment violation.

Moreover, *Right to Read* [109] and *Salvail* [110] from Federal District Courts in the First Circuit Appeals Court jurisdiction prohibited removal of books.

With such a dichotomizing standard—the First, Sixth, and Eighth Circuit Courts of Appeals on one horn and the Second Circuit Court of Appeals occupying the other horn—national judicial continuity is a sparse commodity.

Cary v. Board of Education of Adams-Arapahoe School District

427 F. Supp. 945 (D. Colo. 1977), *aff'd*, 589 F.2d 535 (10th Cir. 1979)

Facts

Five Adams-Arapahoe School District high school English teachers litigated the school board because the board refused to purchase ten books, refused to allow teachers to make assignments in the books and disallowed high school credit for reading the books.

The five high school English teachers taught courses in "Contemporary Literature," "Contemporary Poetry," and

---

108. *Ibid.*

109. Right to Read Defense Comm. v. School Comm., 454 F. Supp. 703 (D. Mass. 1978).

110. Salvail v. Nashua Bd. of Educ., 469 F. Supp. 1269 (D.N.H. 1979).

"American Masters." Of course teachers had been using the banned novels and poetry books in their classes.

What the school board had done was to appoint a review committee, including school board members, teachers, students, and parents. The review committee's charge included an analysis of both current and future books and materials. The committee held a hearing—soliciting comments and views from the entire community. The committee recommended 1,285 books for approval and a single book was rejected. The recommendation was not entirely unanimous—a minority report was filed rejecting nine books. The school board after receiving the report rejected the additional books—approving 1,275 books. Finally, the school board formalized a previous unwritten policy allowing either student and/or parent who objected to an assignment to receive a different one.

Of course plaintiffs—English teachers—insisted that school board actions violated teachers professional constitutional rights to academic freedom. The school board rejected such assertion and maintained that all courses and material were within the school board's scope and authority. Finally, there is another complicating element. The five plaintiffs—English teachers—belong to the Aurora Education Association which was the bargaining agent with the school board in the professional negotiation process. And in the collective bargaining contract was the following sentence "the processes, techniques, methods and means of teaching any and all subjects was a school board privilege."

Decision

The court's homily, with Justice Matsch writing, included a lengthy review of judicial decisions concerning academic freedom. Justice Matsch insisted:

> Academic freedom as the protection of open communication in the processes of teaching does not restrict the public authority to control the educational program and the place where it occurs. We will have such schools operating at such times and place with such curricula as the elected representatives of the people shall determine; but involuntary restrictions on the individual liberty of teachers and students to communicate, directly and indirectly, where such open expression is consistent with the attained level of educational development, are matters of constitutional concern.[111]

But maintained Justice Matsch, academic freedom does not emerge as the central issue in the case at bar. Rather, maintained Justice Matsch, that imperative sentence in the collective bargaining contract emerges as all compelling—the issue becomes one of contract instead of academic freedom. Moreover, continued Justice Matsch, absent the collective bargaining contract then teacher's academic freedom would prevail—"The plaintiffs are bound by that commitment and they may not now seek to avoid it by calling upon a constitutional freedom to act independently and individually." [112] Thus, Justice Matsch ruled in favor of the school board.

On appeal the Tenth Circuit Court of Appeals, with Justice Logan writing the opinion, insisted the district court was in error in determining that the collective bargaining contract was the imperative issue. Continuing, Justice Logan said:

> We thus construe the contract as giving control over textual material to the school board insofar as it can be done consistent with the federal and Colorado Constitutions. We do not construe it to call for waiver of teachers' individual constitutional rights.[113]

---

111. Cary v. Board of Educ., 427 F. Supp, p. 954.

112. *Ibid.*, p. 956.

113. Cary v. Board of Educ., 598 F.2d, p. 539.

So the school board has control over textual material "within" the Federal and Colorado constitutional constraints. This means that a school board could promulgate rules and regulations concerning the use of books. Moreover, teachers could comment on, discuss, or recommend to students any of the ten books. Also outside of class, teachers could meet students any place and any time for book discussion. Students were not prohibited from reading the books except for class credit. Likewise, class discussion of the books was not prohibited except when discussion took excessive time detracting from the objectives of the class. "In short, the proscription relates only to activities which in substance, if not form, would reinstate the nonselected work on the reading list from which it was deliberately removed." [114]

Justice Logan considered the clarification of the school board regulation of great importance. It recognized that teachers' academic freedom and free expression were important rights, but teachers' rights have limits and must be balanced against state authority satisfying the states' compelling interest in education.

Finally, Justice Logan insisted that since the school board had authority to prescribe and select curriculum and materials, the board by the same logic had the authority to exclude materials. Thus, the judicial decision had to be in the school board's favor.

Discussion

This decision differs with other decisions previously discussed because the case deals, in the real sense, with school board authority to delineate use of modern novels and poetry in the classroom rather than in the library. As a matter of fact book banning and the school library was never an issue in this case.

---

114. *Ibid.*, p. 543.

Based on this decision within the Tenth Circuit Court of Appeals jurisdiction school boards may remove and/or prohibit the selection of books because of social or political tastes. However, there is a modifying condition. School board policy with respect to censored books must not restrict out of class reading and in class free discussion. Teachers' academic freedom and constitutional supports must fade as long as school board policies are properly exercised and within the scope and authority proscribed by federal and state constitutional and statutory guidelines.

Bicknell v. Vergennes Union High School Board of Directors

475 F. Supp. 615 (D. Vt. 1979), aff'd,
638 F.2d 438 (2d Cir. 1980)

Facts

This case came on appeal by student plaintiffs and school librarian from the federal district court which had dismissed plaintiffs' complaints that school board had violated their First Amendment rights in removing books from the library and due process rights by revising book removal policy. Justice Albert W. Coffin had dismissed the complaint "for failure to state a claim on which relief can be granted." [115]

Decision

The *Bicknell* and *Pico* courts were made up by the same three justices. Moreover, the two cases were decided on the same day. Justice Newman writing the majority in *Bicknell* had teamed with Justice Sifton to create the majority in *Pico*. In *Bicknell*, Justice Newman teamed with Justice

---

115. Bicknell v. Vergennes Union High School Bd. of Directors, 638 F.2d 438, 440 (2d Cir. 1980).

Mansfield establishing the majority with Justice Sifton filing a dissenting opinion. Justice Mansfield had filed a dissenting opinion in *Pico*.

Thus, Justice Newman insisted that school board action removing the two questionable books for vulgar and indecent language and subsequent altering of book removal policy: (1) did not violate First Amendment rights; (2) school board did not owe students and librarian a due process hearing before book removal; and (3) school board action was not so notorious as to justify a due process hearing for the school librarian.[116]

Discussion

Justice Newman's decision in *Bicknell* realized the Second Circuit Court of Appeals position established in *Presidents Council*. *Pico* is somewhat an aberration but the propinquity of religion and politics had potential for adversion.

At center in *Bicknell* is Board of Directors' action, after parents complaints, removing two books—Patrick Mann's *Dog Day Afternoon* and Richard Price's *The Wanderers* — from the high school library for vulgar and indecent language. Moreover, the Board of Directors voted to disallow school librarian to purchase major fictional works and that all books purchased (except limited science fiction and high interest-low vocabulary) "must be reviewed by the school administration in consultation with the Board." [117]

Plaintiff(s)' litigious protest juxtaposed school board action against school board policy. Because of continuous controversy concerning library books the Board of Directors had established policy entitled the "School Library Bill of

---

116. *Ibid.*, p. 439.
117. *Ibid.*, p. 441.

Rights for School Library Media Center Program." [118] The major policy points are: (1) Board of Directors should develop policy consistent with state statute and otherwise state regulations and also in the best interest of students, parents and professional staff; (2) that professional staff, within limits established by policy, could "freely select . . . organize and administer the media collection to best serve teachers and students"; (3) students may have free access and freely read all library materials; and (4) finally, the policy provided a parent review process for questionable books. [119]

There are two constitutional questions to be considered: (1) was the Board of Directors motivated "solely by the 'personal taste and values'" of its members[120]; and (2) did the Board owe students and school librarian a due process hearing before book removal and did the Board owe due process hearing to students and school librarian because of policy violation? Judge Newman dismissed the first question by insisting that the Board of Directors removed the book because of vulgar and/or indecent language thus no real legal question of the Board's "taste and values." The Board's personal standard concerning vulgar and/or indecent language "is no cause for legal complaint." [121] In response to the second question Justice Newman maintained that students and school librarian, under the circumstances, really have no due process considerations before book removal. Moreover, the school librarian was not harmed in such manner — "The Board did not dismiss her, or reprimand her in any official way"—that required due process protection. [122] Finally, Justice Newman insisted

---

118. *Ibid.*, p. 440.
119. *Ibid.*
120. *Ibid.*, p. 441.
121. *Ibid.*
122. *Ibid.*, p. 442.

that just because the Board did not follow its policy did not "create interests entitled to due process protection." [123] On this last point there would appear to be some difficulty squaring *Bicknell* with *Pico*. But, maintained Justice Newman, *Pico* turns on political and religious concerns and in *Bicknell* "there is no dispute that the two books were removed because of vulgarity and indecency." [124] Justice Sifton filed a dissenting opinion insisting that he saw no real difference—perhaps a distinction without a difference—between *Pico* and *Bicknell*.

§ 4.4. Parents' Right to Direct the Education of Children.

Overview

Parents' right to direct the education of children has been a continuing litigious problem throughout the history of American public education. The United States Supreme Court has addressed this issue on two occasions—*Meyer* [125] and *Yoder* [126] — and in both cases supported parents' rights to direct the education of their children. *Meyer* has already been delineated in this chapter and it is sufficient to remind school boards and school administrators once again that parents have some control over the education of children even when the legislative delegation has enacted legislation encapsulating a specific subject area—prohibited teaching foreign language to students below eighth grade level in either public or private schools. The Supreme Court's reminder that "the power of parents to control the

---

123. *Ibid.*

124. *Ibid.*

125. Meyer v. Nebraska, 262 U.S. 390, 43 S. Ct. 625, 67 L. Ed. 1042 (1923).

126. Wisconsin v. Yoder, 406 U.S. 205, 92 S. Ct. 1526, 32 L. Ed. 2d 15 (1972).

education of their own" cannot be disregarded.[127] *Yoder* is a primary "parents' right" Supreme Court decision and is reviewed below.

As the judicial record establishes that the majority of recent censorship cases have placed emphasis on students' rights instead of parents' rights. There is the exception and the exception encapsulates censorship and religious issues in the curriculum.

The Supreme Court's 1968 *Epperson*[128] decision is the case most often cited in religious censorship cases. The *Todd*[129] and *Medeiros*[130] decisions are representative cases in which parents object to instructional material used in courses on religious grounds. In both cases the court(s) found for the school board(s).

Wisconsin v. Yoder

406 U.S. 205, 92 S. Ct. 1526, 32 L. Ed. 2d 15 (1972)

Facts

Parents, members of the Old Order Amish religion and the Conservative Amish Mennonite Church, refused to send their fourteen- and fifteen-year-old children to school beyond the eighth grade. Wisconsin's compulsory attendance law required children to attend school until the age of sixteen. Of course the parents were charged and convicted, in a lower court, of violating the compulsory attendance law.

The Amish people provided children with a continuing vocational education in order to prepare them for life in the

---

127. Meyer v. Nebraska, 262 U.S., p. 401.

128. Epperson v. Arkansas, 393 U.S. 97, 89 S. Ct. 266, 21 L. Ed. 2d 228 (1968).

129. Todd v. Rochester Community Schools, 41 Mich. App. 320, 200 N.W.2d 90 (1972).

130. Medeiros v. Kiyosaki, 52 Hawaii 436, 478 P.2d 314 (1970).

rural community in which they lived. Moreover, parents insisted that high school attendance was contrary to the Amish religion and way of life. Secondary school attendance, suggested parents, endangered salvation for both parents and children.

Decision

The Wisconsin Supreme Court sustained defendants' claims of First Amendment religious freedom violation. On certiorari, the United States Supreme Court affirmed the decision six to three.

Chief Justice Warren Burger writing the majority maintained that:

1. The Amish people and religion sincerely opposed secondary schooling because of worldly influences children would be exposed to "in terms of attitudes, goals, and values." [131] Secondary school exposure would substantially interfere with integrating children into the mainstream of Amish life and faith at the crucial adolescent stage of childhood development.

2. Moreover, foregoing one or two years of compulsory education would not: (1) impair students' physical and/or mental health; (2) result in students' inability to be self-supporting; (3) prevent children from fulfilling citizenship responsibilities; nor (4) materially detract from the general welfare of society. The states compelling interest in education did not outweigh the age long established religious practices of the Amish people.

3. Finally, Justice Burger suggested that Amish parents had been prosecuted because their children did not attend school. The record also indicates that children

---

131. Wisconsin v. Yoder, 406 U.S., p. 205.

supported parents wishes; at least to the extent that students did not protest parents' decision. Parents' First Amendment religious freedom exercise becomes the prime mover in this decision.

Discussion

This decision certainly supports parents' insistence to direct the education of their children. Justice Burger insisted that the state's compelling interest in education was satisfied with an eighth grade education in so far as the Amish First Amendment religious freedom was concerned. Of course Justice Burger conditioned the decision with the aged Amish history which theoretically other religions would have to substantially match in order to similarly qualify. School boards and school administrators should certainly heed this clarion decision when the possibilities of school board curriculum policies and/or materials used are on a collision course with an age-old established religion and religious practices.

Epperson v. Arkansas

393 U.S. 97, 89 S. Ct. 266, 21 L. Ed. 2d 228 (1968)

Overview

This landmark Supreme Court decision insisted that Arkansas legislative enactment prohibiting teaching the theory of evolution was unconstitutional. This decision is almost always referred to in judicial decisions concerning First Amendment religious establishment violations and First Amendment free speech and communication abridgment.

Facts

An Arkansas public school biology teacher litigated the state statute which prohibited the teaching in state supported elementary and secondary schools and universities of the Darwin's theory of evolution. Furthermore, textbook

190

adoption which included the Darwinian theory was also prohibited. The teacher was scheduled to use a newly adopted biology textbook that included a chapter concerning Darwinian theory of evolution. Violation of the state statute was a misdemeanor and teachers were subject to dismissal. The teacher was joined by a parent in the litigation.

Plaintiffs challenged the constitutionality of the anti-evolution statute which was in essence based on the 1925 Tennessee "monkey law." The Arkansas Chancery Court insisted the statute violated the Fourteenth Amendment of the Constitution. On appeal the Arkansas Supreme Court reversed the decision. The Arkansas Supreme Court maintained that the statute was a legitimate exercise of state authority to prescribe curriculum in public schools. On appeal the United States Supreme Court reversed the Arkansas Supreme Court seven to two on First and Fourteenth Amendment grounds.

Decision

Justice Abe Fortas delivered the Court's decision. Justice Fortas' commentary included "[p]lainly the law is contrary to the mandate of the First and in violation of the Fourteenth Amendment to the Constitution." [132] Continuing, Justice Fortas maintained that:

1. State and the Federal government must remain neutral in religious theory, doctrine and practices. Government may not aid, foster, or promote one religion or religious theory over another. Government may neither oppose religion nor advocate non-religion.

2. That courts are reluctant to interfere with the daily operation of public schools. However, where there is violation of basic constitutional values the judiciary

---

132. Epperson v. Arkansas, 393 U.S., p. 109.

must intrude. " 'Laws that cast a pall of orthodoxy over the classroom' " are a violation of the freedom-of-religion provision of the First Amendment and therefore they cannot be tolerated.[133]

3. The Supreme Court is always concerned with the invasion of academic freedom.

4. Study of the Bible and religions from a historical and literary viewpoint is a legitimate exercise of the secular program of education. However, the First Amendment insists that states may not adopt curriculum programs and/or practices that foster or oppose any religion.

5. Finally, the state's authority to prescribe curricula does not include punishing teachers, on pain of criminal penalty, if the prohibiting—in this case teaching Darwin's theory of evolution — is flawed with First Amendment violations.

Discussion

The *Epperson* decision is a prime example of the Supreme Court response to censorship by legislative fiat. While the Arkansas General Assembly legislative action is the focal point of *Epperson* other states throughout America's history have enacted "Genesis" statutes. Thus, whenever there are legislative imperatives, school board policies, and/or school administrator discretion encapsulating religion and the education process—irrespective of the complainant—the *Epperson* dictum provides judicial guidelines for cutting the constitutional Gordian knot.

Finally, in early 1981 the Arkansas General Assembly enacted another "Genesis" statute known as the "balance treatment statute." The statute required that balance treatment be presented when teaching human

---

133. *Ibid.*, p. 105.

origins—balance treatment between scientific evolution theory and scientific creationism. Already a Federal District Court in Little Rock has declared the statute unconstitutional as First Amendment religious advancement—a "Genesis" statute in any form is still a "Genesis" statute.[134] At this writing there are some nineteen other states with similar legislative proposals. Louisiana's General Assembly has enacted a balanced treatment statute into law.

Earlier, in the manuscript this form of government activity was described as censorship by "benign neglect." The *Epperson* Court stripped any shred of scientific respectability away from "balance treatment statutes" easily recognizing that censorship in any form — "benign neglect"—is still censorship and a constitutional violation as First Amendment establishment of religion.

Medeiros v. Kiyosaki

52 Hawaii 436, 478 P.2d 314 (1970)

Facts

A family life and sex education program was adopted by the State of Hawaii. The State Superintendent of Education, upon recommendation from the Department of Education staff selected a film series, "Time of Your Life," to be used with the curriculum. The film series was initially developed for educational television and previously used in San Francisco. The film package consisted of fifteen lessons, covering inter-personal relationships, self-understanding, family structure, and sex education. Lessons eleven through fifteen covered sexuality and sexual development

---

134. McLean v. Arkansas Bd. of Educ., 529 F. Supp. 1255 (E.D. Ark. 1982).

and supplemented classroom lessons planned by the teacher for fifth- and sixth-grade students. Parents could request that children be excused from the lessons.

Parents of fifth- and sixth-grade students claimed that viewing the films interfered with parents' rights to educate their children in matters of sex and thus violated constitutional right to privacy and religious freedom.

Decision

The First City and County Circuit Court of Honolulu dismissed the complaint, and it was appealed to the Supreme Court of Hawaii.

The Hawaii Supreme Court with Chief Justice Richardson writing the opinion affirmed the lower court, maintaining:

1. Fifth- and sixth-grade students "optional excuse" from participation in the film series upon parents' request negated parents' constitutional protest concerning privacy.
2. Moreover, because of the "optional excuse" feature there was no First Amendment free religious exercise violation.
3. State boards of education have broad discretionary powers in establishing curricula and instituting educational programs in the state's public schools.
4. The film series of family life and sex education had been properly adopted by the state board of education.

Discussion

The *Medeiros* homily provides common sense guidelines for school boards and school administrators: (1) in sensitive areas of family life and sex education policy safeguards must be established buffering parents' constitutional right to privacy and First Amendment free religious exercise; and (2) an appropriate policy was developed and was precisely followed in selection of instructional material in sensitive curriculum areas.

Todd v. Rochester Community Schools

41 Mich. App. 320, 200 N.W.2d 90 (1972)

Facts

The parent of a high school student complained that use of Kurt Vonnegut's novel *Slaughterhouse-Five,* in an elective current literature course violated First and Fourteenth Amendment rights. The complaint maintained the book made reference to religious matters therefore violating the First Amendment religious establishment clause.

The Michigan trial court insisted the book could be removed from the school library. Further, the book should not be promoted and/or recommended reading in any courses of study.

Decision

On appeal the Michigan Appeals Court, with Justice Bronson writing the opinion, reversed the lower court's decision. The trial court had predicated the decision primarily on *Schempp.*[135] *Schempp* was an erroneous anchor and inapplicable, insisted Justice Bronson. Although the trial court never declared the book obscene the possibility was suggested. Justice Bronson, responding to the obscene issue, manifestly insisted the book was not obscene when measured against any constitutional test. Furthermore, insisted Justice Bronson, the trial court in imposing the court's judgement on the citizenry had abused judicial discretion by entering a traditionally sacred area.

---

135. School Dist. of Abington Township v. Schempp, 374 U.S. 203, 83 S. Ct. 1560, 10 L. Ed. 2d 844 (1963).

Justice Bronson asserted that whatever religious use derived from the novel did not violate the First Amendment religious establishment clause. Justice Bronson echoed a continuous judicial refrain—although public schools may teach about religion they may not teach religion.

Finally, Justice Bronson, in finding for the school board, said:

> It is for the lawfully elected school board, its supervisory personnel and its teachers to determine a local public schools' curriculum; the judicial censors are a persona non grata in formation of public education.[136]

Discussion

This decision establishes once again that the majority of courts will support school board policies. Courts are very reluctant to intervene in day-to-day school operation. This decision continues the prevailing judicial position—schools may not teach religion; however, when religious issues emerge from the literature teachers may discuss the religious issue.

Kurt Vonnegut's novel *Slaughterhouse-Five* was never declared obscene. Once again, in this case as in the majority of judicial decisions the obscenity issue never emerged. Likewise, parents' personal philosophies and/or religious propensities juxtaposed with religious discussion did not establish a constitutional issue.

---

136. Todd v. Rochester Community Schools, 200 N.W.2d, p. 90.

Chapter 5

SUMMARY, CONCLUSIONS, AND RECOMMENDATIONS

§ 5.0. Summary.
§ 5.1. Conclusions.
§ 5.2. Recommendations.
§ 5.3. Concluding Statement.
§ 5.4. Recommended School Board Policy for Selection of Library and Instructional Materials.

Throughout the history of American public education, censorship of school library and instructional materials has been a continuous issue for school boards, school administrators, teachers, and librarians. Based on an analysis of research presented in this study, it is apparent that censorship involving public schools is a growing concern. Moreover, any level of public education may be confronted with controversy concerning library books, films, periodicals, instructional materials, or matters involving curricula.

Prevailing social, political, moral, and religious trends which influence community pressures on schools may lead to a censorship controversy. The censor may be a parent, a member of the community, a local or national organization, a student, a teacher, a librarian, a principal, a superintendent, or even a school board. Censorship attempts may or may not be settled to the satisfaction of the complainant, the community or the school board. As the school board appeals process is exhausted, resolution may require litigation.

Censorship involves major constitutional issues such as academic freedom, students' rights, parents' right to direct the education of children, religious freedom, and the authority of school administrators and school boards. Therefore, school officials should have access to appropriate

197

information concerning both the educational and legal issues related to censorship in order to make sound educational and legal decisions. The comprehensive summaries of recent studies regarding censorship and identification of potentially litigious educational issues provided by this research may assist school officials in making sound educational decisions where censorship is concerned.

§ 5.0. Summary.

The introductory material in Chapter 1 identified the historical fact that censorship is an ancient problem. However, public schools have been faced with more censorship problems and litigation concerning censorship in the past two decades than ever before in the history of the United States. The current political, social, and moral climate is central to understanding the basis for censorship of school library and instructional materials. Citizens' dissatisfaction with forced desegregation, busing, taxes, foreign policy, and government in general has caused them to strike out at public schools. Propinquity and familiarity make the school an easier target than federal, state, or local governments. Well-organized groups, some conservative, some liberal, have been formed to lead various school censorship movements.

Reiterating a statement made in the overview of Chapter 2, "Review of Related Literature," no attempt was made to include an exhaustive review of censorship. Instead, an historical perspective was presented to give the reader background and a world overview of the subject. Selected key studies were presented in an effort to clarify the complexity of the basic judicial considerations contained in the court cases presented in Chapters 3 and 4.

As a guide to the educational and legal research, several questions were formulated and listed in Chapter 1 of this study. While the review of the literature provided answers to some of these questions, most of the answers were contained in Chapters 3 and 4. The answers to these questions comprise the major portion of a set of legal guidelines which school administrators and other educational decision makers can refer to when making decisions related to censorship.

The first question listed in Chapter 1 was: Under what circumstances will constitutional rights of students, teachers, or parents be involved when a school district is faced with a censorship problem?

I. Constitutional rights of students become involved in censorship problems

    A. when there is removal of and/or limited access to library and instructional materials, thus inhibiting students' right to read, to learn, or to receive information.

    B. when assignments to use specific books and materials are deemed to conflict with any student's moral or religious values, particularly when no provision has been made for an alternative assignment or excuse policy.

II. Constitutional rights of teachers become involved

    A. when library books or instructional materials are proscribed in violation of professional constitutionally based academic freedoms.

    B. when teachers are suspended or dismissed because of using controversial materials, thus violating First Amendment rights to academic freedom or Fourteenth Amendment liberty and property interest to hold a position.

III. Constitutional rights of parents become involved in censorship

    A. when students receive assignments, without an alternative assignment or excuse policy, deemed to interfere with

1. the parents' right to determine the education of their children.
2. the moral and religious beliefs of the parents.
3. the privacy of the family.

The second question posed in the introductory chapter was related to identifying the major educational issues involving censorship of library and instructional materials.

The major educational issues are

I. conflict between the "indoctrination" theory of education, fostering the transmission of traditional values and community mores, as opposed to the contemporary educational view of the school as a marketplace of ideas.

II. ultraconservative pressures on school boards, and school administrators which oppose teaching young people everything from various political or economic theories, scientific theories, world religions, or information concerning ethnic groups, to teaching them the new themes in modern literature.

III. pressure groups which demand that schools prohibit any type of "sexism" or "racism" in teaching or literature.

IV. emerging students' rights from judicial decisions, predicated on Constitutional interpretation giving students more decision-making opportunities in their own education.

V. teachers' increasing rights to academic freedom allowing them to make more decisions concerning classroom instruction and the books and materials supporting the teaching role, as opposed to authority of school boards to prescribe curricula and select instructional material.

VI. the judicial determination of an appropriate selection procedure so that the wise choice of library and instructional materials will meet the educational needs of students without unduly antagonizing parents, the community, or pressure groups.

VII. organization and governance of schools by school boards and administrators who have sound educational philosophies, objectives, and policies and are willing to support such beliefs under fire from a variety of pressure groups.

VIII. the use of family life and sex education programs in public schools.

IX. the ability of school systems to win and hold community support in the task of educating young people for whom they are responsible.

The third question listed in Chapter 1 concerns the pressure groups chiefly responsible for censorship. The main group of censors consists of parents. However, librarians, school administrators, and school boards also become censors when parent and community pressure is brought to bear on them.

Many parents who become censors assume the role from genuine personal concern based on moral, religious, and political and social convictions. Others are influenced by a large number of highly organized national and local groups formed for the explicit purpose of "cleansing" the public schools. These groups have large mailing lists through which they circulate information concerning "objectionable" textbooks, library books, and other instructional materials. The same organizations also send out information protesting specific school programs such as family life and sex education curricula, humanities programs, the teaching of Darwin's theory of evolution, and values clarification. These groups often appear to be motivated mainly from moral and/or religious convictions. The end result of such groups and supporting ideology, coupled with national social trends, is that many "Christian Academies" have emerged in which there is a presumption that children can get religious training unavailable in public schools.

201

In the decade of the eighties ultraconservative groups frequently consist of blending fundamentalist religion and political conservatism into a working personal philosophy. These groups customarily oppose federal legislation such as abortion laws, the Equal Rights Amendment, school integration, the high cost of school programs, and similar issues. Moreover, they often excoriate specific educational philosophies of public schools. All individuals and pressure groups have concerns, the amelioration of which requires capable school administrators who can respond effectively to individual and organized pressure. The ability to mold public support with honest, effective tools and planning is an essential skill for current school administrators and school boards.

The fourth guide question from Chapter 1 concerned specific trends determined from an analysis of court cases relating to censorship. The final guide question was related to legally acceptable criteria, based on landmark cases, most likely to assist school districts in preventing legal action and/or poor public relations in the event of censorship cases. The answers to these two questions, as revealed by an analysis of the literature and judicial decisions, provide the framework for the "Conclusions" and "Recommendations" sections of this study.

§ 5.1. Conclusions.

Even when legal issues appear to be similar and/or the same as those in cases already decided by the courts, a different set of circumstances can produce an entirely different decision. Thus, drawing specific conclusions from legal research is difficult. However, based on an analysis of judicial decisions, the following general conclusions can be made concerning the legal aspects of censorship of school library and instructional materials.

1. Courts will intervene in the educational decision-making prerogatives of local school officials only if an individual's constitutionally protected right has allegedly been denied because of censorship action.

2. Judicial conceptualization of constitutionally protected rights will continue to be a challenging philosophical mandate for the courts.

3. Definition of elementary and secondary schools as places for the indoctrination of community mores, as opposed to their being a "marketplace of ideas," will continue as a legal issue to be grappled with by the courts.

4. The scope of academic freedom for elementary and secondary public school teachers will continue to be an issue for exploration and investigation by courts.

5. The direction and extent of students' rights to receive information in elementary and secondary public schools will likely be a protracted area of judicial investigation.

6. School boards' authority to remove library and instructional materials, as opposed to the selection of the same materials, will continue to have judicial scrutinization.

7. Parents' constitutional rights to determine the course of education of their children in the public schools, as opposed to school board authority and professional staff judgement to prescribe curricula, will likely continue to be litigated.

8. With the current renewal of fundamentalist religious philosophies and traditional moralism, questions relating to the use of various library and instructional materials will be issues for judicial determination.

9. Conflicting findings in at least five Circuit Courts, the First, Second, Sixth, Seventh, and Eighth Circuit Courts, suggest that the United States Supreme Court provide definitive guidelines concerning censorship in the public schools. The *Pico* decision, at this time, does not appear to be a definitive case.

10. None of the library and instructional materials questioned in any of the cases studied were declared legally obscene when evaluated within the conceptual framework of the *Miller* Test.

11. The judicial trend has always been in favor of school boards especially when sound policies have been formed and explicitly followed.

§ 5.2. Recommendations.

The stated purpose of this study was to provide educational decision makers with appropriate information regarding the legal aspects of censorship of school library and instructional materials so that they might be able to make educationally and legally sound decisions concerning the issues.

The current political and religious climate seems to point toward a trend for continued examination and criticism of public school library and instructional materials. Capable and skilled educators will be required, in order to gain community support, to withstand pressure from a variety of citizens and national and local organizations. In a democracy citizens have the right to express views and raise important questions concerning public education. Educators must develop organizational and administrative activities that will keep the public informed about schooling and generate public support.

Moreover, educators should continue to be informed and keep up to date with respect to constitutional issues and legal developments affecting schools. Lack of legal knowledge is no longer an acceptable excuse for arbitrary or capricious policies and/or activities. Special caution should be taken to prevent violation of constitutionally protected rights of teachers, students, school employees, and parents. School board policies must be legally formulated, adopted, and implemented. A carefully designed, written plan for selection of library books and instructional materials should be adopted and explicitly followed. The same is true for the handling of complaints concerning such materials.

Upon adoption of school board policy a thorough staff development plan should be implemented. All professional staff and school board members should participate in the workshop. There must be complete understanding of school board policy as well as censorship pressures. Any school board capitulating to censorship by a particular pressure group must face the possibility that surrender could result in encouragement of pressure from other groups, thus leading to confusion and interference in the educational process. Moreover, such a capitulatory position frequently invites litigation from another segment of the society—the American Civil Liberty Union. These cautionary practices should assist school boards in avoiding litigation and improving community relationships.

Finally, with *Pico* and *Pratt* as the guideline, school boards and school administrators must not allow political and religious pressure groups to co-opt policy and curriculum desecration.

The struggle for authority and control of people's minds and souls is always omnipresent. Arrogance, ignorance, dogma, and absolute knowledge are the descriptive words in this struggle. But in a democracy it is not the purpose of school boards to control the minds and souls of students and teachers. Rather, it is the purpose of school boards to provide such a stimulating academic atmosphere that students learn how to "think." Of course teaching students how to "think" — "a market place of ideas" — that collides with the concept of what the student must think about — "the indoctrination process"—is always the litigious issue.

Based on the results of this study, the following guidelines concerning censorship of school library and instructional materials have been formulated. These guidelines are based on the legal principles established by the United States Supreme Court landmark decisions and on discernible trends revealed by the numerous lower federal court decisions in cases related to these practices. While these appear to be legally acceptable criteria to follow, school officials need to remember that individuals who feel their constitutional rights have been abridged may still initiate judicial grievances.

Guidelines for a Policy
Concerning Selection and Withdrawal of
School Library and Instructional Materials

I. All school board policies concerning selection and/or removal of library and instructional materials should have formal approval of the school board. Some suggestions follow:

    A. A written plan which includes a philosophy and objectives of the libraries and the instruction program of the school district as well as a detailed plan for handling complaints.

    B. The policy should begin with a statement that the school board intends to protect the constitutional rights of students, parents, and school personnel in every circumstance.

    C. The development of the statement should be done in conjunction with librarians, teachers, administrators, students, and knowledgeable parents.

    D. The policy statement should include an expansion of the legislative concept that all rules of the school board are intended to be fair, reasonable, and for the good of schools and students.

    E. The policy should state clearly that while the school board has the right and duty to establish policies, such policies are not absolute.

F. The executive dimension of the policy statement should be clear with the intent of applying policies and rules equally to everyone and that no discrimination nor application inconsistent with the policy will be tolerated.

II. These additional topics should be covered by the school board policy:

A. The most fundamental concept in formulating the school board policy is the selection or removal of library and instructional materials at the school level. For this reason the policy should state clearly the procedures to be followed in the selection and removal process at the school level. The following are suggestions:

1. A school library/media selection committee should be established in each school. It should be composed of the principal or his designee, the librarian or a professional member of the library staff, a member of the supervisory staff, teachers representing the different areas of the curriculum, qualified parents, and, if the maturity level is appropriate, students.

2. The school library/media selection committee should adopt a philosophy and objectives consistent with that of the school and the school district.

3. Criteria for judging books and materials should be established.

4. Specific procedures and selection aids should be designated for use in the selecting process, covering the broad areas to be served by the curriculum, the objectives of the school, and the needs and interests of students. Selection aids should be professionally prepared,

207

unbiased, and reputable. Materials should be examined first-hand whenever possible.

5. A procedure for accepting gifts of books and materials should be included so that they meet the same criteria as other materials selected for the library collection.

6. Guidelines for discarding worn, obsolete, or damaged books and materials should be included.

7. A plan concerning the replacement of worn, missing, or damaged materials should be developed.

B. Procedures for reconsideration of materials and handling complaints should be carefully drawn. These should apply equally to all complaints whether they be from school personnel, parents, students, or other citizens.

1. Complaints should be initiated at the particular school or library where the complaint has been received. If a school board member or superintendent receives a complaint then that complaint should be referred to the particular school whenever possible. The school library/media selection committee should constitute the first level of appeal.

2. Prepare a form to be filled out by any complainant. The form should be readily accessible in the library or principal's office at all times.

3. Inform the complainant of selection procedures. Make no comments or commitments concerning the materials to which there is objection.

4. Invite the complainant to complete the form in writing so that it may be formally reviewed.

C. If the problem is not satisfactorily settled at the school level, the superintendent should appoint a review committee made up of professional educators in the school district, representatives of school/library selection committee where the complaint was initiated, and other appropriate citizens. Review by this committee should constitute the second level of appeal. The responsibilities of this committee should be clearly stated.

  1. The challenged material should be examined.

  2. Evaluations of challenged material should be surveyed in professional reviewing sources.

  3. Determine the extent to which the material supports the curriculum and the philosophy and objectives of the school district.

  4. Weigh merits against alleged faults in order to form opinions based on the material as a whole rather than through passages isolated from context.

  5. Prepare a written recommendation to the superintendent and school board.

D. If the controversy is unsettled at the review committee level then, the school board should be the third and final level of appeal through the school district.

§ 5.3. Concluding Statement.

If a school district becomes involved in censorship controversy, a conscientious attempt should be made to resolve the problem through school board policy and action. If such procedure is unsuccessful, a high probability exists that litigation will be initiated either by an individual student, a group of students, teachers, parents, or concerned citizens or whomever. Courts will not usually hear censorship cases unless local appeal procedures have been exhausted.

If the complainant can establish that the school board and/or administrators arbitrarily deprived him of a constitutional right, he may be able to receive financial remuneration under the Civil Rights Act of 1971 (G.S. 1983) from individual school board members and school administrators.

No school board policy or guidelines will guarantee in perpetuity the absence of litigation by individuals or groups who maintain their rights have been violated. However, school boards and school administrators can reduce the probability of having school practices litigated (and thus no financial liability) by formulating, implementing, and explicitly following a set of guidelines governing the selection and removal of library and instructional materials.

§ 5.4. Recommended School Board Policy for Selection of Library and Instructional Materials.

I. *Statement of Policy.*

The Board of Education of the _____ _____ School District has been authorized by the State Legislature of _____, (Statute No.) with the responsibility for providing library and instructional materials for the school district. In this, as in all other endeavors, the Board of Education strives to meet the educational needs of students and the instructional needs of the staff fairly, reasonably, and judiciously, with the best interests of students and the schools as first priority. The intent of the school board is to protect the constitutional rights of students, parents, and school personnel in every circumstance. Policies apply equally to all persons involved. No discrimination nor inconsistent application will be tolerated. The Board of Education has the authority and the duty to make policies; however, policies may be revised, added, or eliminated when circumstances necessitate such action.

II. *Responsibility for Selection of Materials.*

The Board of Education delegates authority for selection of library and instructional materials through the Superintendent of Schools to school library/media selection committees under the guidance of professionally trained librarians and the Coordinator of School Libraries.

The following procedures shall be followed:
A. Each school shall establish a library/media selection committee appointed by the principal and composed of (1) the school principal or his designee, (2) the school librarian as chairman of the committee, and (3) teachers representing all areas of the curriculum and/or grade levels. The principal may also appoint one or more community representatives, and, if the maturity level is appropriate, students.
B. Under the leadership of the library/media personnel the selection committee shall set priorities for acquisition of materials based on school-wide objectives, the strengths and weaknesses of the existing collection, and budget allocations.

III. *Objectives for Selection.*

The primary objective of the school library/media program is to support, enrich, and help implement the instructional program of the school. It is the duty of the professional staff to make available a wide range of materials of varying levels of difficulty, with a diversity of appeal, and the presentation of different points of view. To this end, the _____ Board of Education in keeping with ideas expressed in the LIBRARY BILL OF RIGHTS, asserts that the responsibility of its professional staff is:
A. To provide materials that will enrich and support the curriculum, taking into consideration individual needs and varied interests, abilities, learning styles, and maturity levels of the students served.

211

B. To provide materials that stimulate growth in factual knowledge, literary appreciation, aesthetic values, and ethical standards.

C. To provide materials on various sides of controversial issues so that young citizens may have an opportunity to develop, under guidance, the practice of critical analysis and to make informed judgments in their daily lives.

D. To provide materials representative of the many religious, ethnic, and cultural groups in our nation and the contributions of these groups to our American heritage and the world community.

E. To place principle above personal opinion and reason above prejudice in selection of materials of the highest quality in order to assure a comprehensive collection appropriate to the school, the community, and the students who use the library.

IV. *Procedures for Selection of Materials.*

A. Instructional materials shall support and be consistent with the general educational goals of the state, the school district, and the aims and objectives of individual schools and specific courses. All materials selected shall meet high standards of quality as outlined in the Manual of Policies and Procedures for School Libraries in the _____ School District. The sources to be consulted are bibliographies and reviewing aids as outlined in the Manual of Policies and Procedures. Whenever possible materials should be examined firsthand.

B. Gift materials should be evaluated through the same criteria as any new materials selected for the collection. The right is reserved to include only those materials which meet these specified criteria.

212

V. *Discarding, Weeding, and Replacing Materials in the Collection.*

 A. Worn, obsolete, and inoperable materials should be continuously discarded from the collection.

 B. Worn, damaged, or missing materials basic to the collection should be replaced as soon as possible.

VI. *Procedures for Reconsideration of Materials.*

Occasional objections to some materials may be voiced despite the care taken in the selection and the qualification of the personnel selecting materials. The following procedures apply equally to all complaints whether they be from students, parents, school personnel, or other citizens.*

 A. Complaints should be presented to the principal or librarian at the school from which the material was received.

 B. The complainant will be asked to fill out a form entitled, "Request for Reconsideration of Educational Materials."

 C. The challenged material will be placed on a reserve shelf where it may be checked out by students with parent's permission until a decision is made.

 D. The school library/media selection committee will review the material and present a written report to the superintendent. The superintendent may accept the report and present it to the complainant. This constitutes the first level of appeal.

 E. The superintendent or the complainant may reject the report of the school library/media committee and move to the second level of appeal. In such case the superintendent, with approval of the school board,

---

* Portions of the policy are based on sample policies from the American Library Association and the Division of Educational Media, North Carolina State Department of Education.

should appoint a review committee made of professional educators in the school district, representatives of the school library/media selection committee where the complaint originated, and other appropriate citizens. The superintendent will present the report to the complainant in writing. This constitutes the second level of appeal.

F. The complainant has the right to appeal any decision to the Board of Education for final review. This constitutes the third and final level of appeal through the school district.

Request for Reconsideration of Educational Materials

Name of complainant _____

Address of complainant _____

Telephone Number _____

In which school was the material to which you object located? _____

_____

Specify type of material _____

book, film, filmstrip, recording, etc.

Author, composer, etc. _____

Publisher or Producer (if known) _____

Who do you represent? _____

yourself, name of organization or identity of group

_____

Have you read, viewed, or listened to the entire item?

_____

yes or no

Did you find anything good about the item? If so, please state: _____

_____

Why do you object to the item? _____

_____

214

What do you feel might be the result of reading, viewing, or listening to the item? _____

_____

Are you aware of the evaluation of this item by authoritative sources?

_____

yes or no

Please cite specific pages, passages, or themes you find objectionable:

_____

_____

Would you recommend this item for any particular age group? If so please state: _____

What would you like your school to do about the item?

    ____Do not assign to my child

    ____Do not assign to any student

    ____Refer to the media review committee for evaluation

    ____Withdraw (ban) it from use in the school system

_____   _____

        Signature   Date

BIBLIOGRAPHY

Books

Alexander, M. David. "First Amendment: Curriculum, Libraries, and Textbooks," pp. 154-62. In *School Law in Contemporary Society*. Edited by M. A. McGhehy. Topeka, Kansas: National Organization on Legal Problems of Education, 1980.

Anderson, A. J. *Problems in Intellectual Freedom and Censorship*. New York: R. R. Bowker Company, 1974.

Anderson, Archibald W. "The 'Nation' Cause." In *The First Freedom: Liberty and Justice in the World of Books and Reading*, pp. 353-59. Edited by Robert B. Downs. Chicago: American Library Association, 1960.

Barker, Lucius J. and Barker, Twiley W., Jr. *Civil Liberties and the Constitution*. Englewood Cliffs, New Jersey: Prentice-Hall, 1975.

Barth, Roland S. *Open Education and the American School*. New York: Agathon Press, 1972.

Beale, Howard K. *A History of Freedom of Teaching in American Schools*. Report of the Commission on the Social Studies, Part XVI. New York: Octagon Books, 1974.

Blanshard, Paul. *The Right to Read: The Battle Against Censorship*. Boston: Beacon Press, 1955.

Bok, Curtis. "Commonwealth v. Gordon et al." In *The First Freedom: Liberty and Justice in the World of Books and Reading*. Edited by Robert B. Downs. Chicago: American Library Association, 1960.

Bolmeier, Edward C. *The School in the Legal Structure*. Second Edition. Cincinnati: H.W. Anderson Company, 1973.

Boyer, Paul S. *Purity in Print: The Vice Society Movement*

and Book Censorship in America. New York: Charles Scribner and Sons, 1968.

Boynton, Percy H. *Literature and American Life.* Boston: Ginn and Company, 1936.

Bronowski, Jacob. *The Ascent of Man.* Boston: Little, Brown and Company, 1973, pp. 196, 199.

Bryson, Joseph E. *Legality of Loyalty Oath and Non-Oath Requirements for Public School Teachers.* Ashville, North Carolina: The Miller Printing Company, 1963.

Burke, Redmond A. *What Is the Index?* Milwaukee: Brace Publishing Company, 1952.

Burress, Lee. "A Brief Report of the 1977 NCTE Censorship Survey." In *Dealing with Censorship,* pp. 14-47. Edited by James E. Davis. Urbana, Illinois: National Council of Teachers of English, 1979.

Chaffee, Zechariah, Jr. *Documents of Fundamental Human Rights.* New York: Atheneum, 1963.

Cohen, Monroe C., ed. *Personal Liberty and Education.* New York: Citation Press, 1976.

Copernicus, Nicolaus. *The Revolution of Heavenly Spheres.* University of Chicago, Great Books of the Western World, Encyclopaedia Britannica, Inc. Robert M. Hutchins, Editor in Chief, 1952, Volume 16, pp. 499-837.

Cremin, Laurence A. *The Transformation of the School.* New York: Alfred A. Knoft, 1961, pp. 58-90.

Davis, James E., ed. *Dealing with Censorship.* Urbana, Illinois: National Council of Teachers of English, 1979.

De Grazia, Edward. *Censorship Landmarks.* New York: Bowker Company, 1969.

Downs, Robert B., ed. *The First Freedom: Liberty and Justice in the World of Books and Reading.* Chicago: American Library Association, 1962.

Educational Policies Commission. *The Central Purpose of*

American Education. Washington, D. C.: National
Education Association, 1962.

Ernst, Morris L. and Schwartz, Alan U. *Censorship: The
Search for the Obscene.* New York: Macmillan, 1964.

Ernst, Morris L. and Seagle, William. *To the Pure . . . A
Study of Obscenity and the Censor.* New York: Viking,
1928.

Farrington, Benjamin. *Greek Science.* London: Penguin,
1953.

Ford, Worthington C. *Boston Book Market, 1697-1700.*
Boston: The Club of Odd Volumes, 1917.

Fuller, B.A.G. *A History of Philosophy.* New York: Henry
Holt and Company, 1945.

Galilei, Galileo. *Dialogue of the Two New Sciences.* Univer-
sity of Chicago, Great Books of the Western World,
Encyclopaedia Britannica, Inc. Robert M. Hutchins,
Editor in Chief, 1952, Volume 28, pp. 127-250.

Gillett, Charles Ripley. *Burned Books: Neglected Chapters
in British History and Literature.* 2 volumes. New
York: Columbia University Press, 1932.

Haight, Anne Lyon. *Banned Books: Informal Notes on Some
Banned for Various Reasons at Various Times and in
Various Places.* New York: Bowker, 1970.

Haney, Robert W. *Comstockery in America: Patterns of
Censorship and Control.* Boston: Beacon Press, 1960.

Hatcher, Thomas C. "Educational Directions in a
Pluralistic Society." In *Indoctrinate or Educate?* pp.
38-41. Edited by Thomas C. Hatcher and Lawrence G.
Erickson. Newark, Delaware: International Reading
Association, 1979.

Hefley, James C. *Textbooks on Trial.* Wheaton, Illinois:
Victor Books, 1976.

Hogan, John C. *The Schools, the Courts, and the Public*

219

Interest. Lexington, Massachusetts: Lexington Books, 1974.

Holt, John. *How Children Fail.* New York: Dell, 1965.

Holy Bible, R.S.V. Jeremiah 35:9-12. New York: Thomas Nelson and Sons, 1952.

Jenkinson, Edward B. "Dirty Dictionaries, Obscene Nursery Rhymes, and Burned Books." In *Dealing with Censorship,* pp. 2-13. Edited by James E. Davis. Urbana, Illinois: National Council of Teachers of English, 1979.

Kalkhoff, Ann. "Innocent Children or Innocent Librarians." In *Issues in Children's Book Selection: A School Library Journal/Library Journal Anthology,* pp. 11-19. New York: R. R. Bowker Company, 1973.

Kennedy, Renick C. "Alabama Book Toasters." In *The First Freedom: Liberty and Justice in the World of Books and Reading,* pp. 375-77. Edited by Robert B. Downs. Chicago: American Library Association, 1960.

Kohl, Herbert R. *The Open Classroom: A Practical Guide to a New Way of Teaching.* New York: Random House, 1969.

Lewis, Felice Flanery. *Literature, Obscenity, and Law.* Carbondale and Edwardsville: Southern Illinois Press, 1976.

Mayer, Frederick. *A History of Modern Philosophy.* New York, American Company, 1951, pp. 65-69.

Milton, John. *Paradise Lost and Selected Poetry and Prose.* Edited by Northrop Frye. New York: Rinehart and Company, 1951.

Moon, Eric, ed. *Book Selection and Censorship in the Sixties.* New York: Bowker, 1969.

Nelson, Jack and Roberts, Gene, Jr. *The Censors and the Schools.* Boston: Little, Brown and Company, 1963.

Oboler, Eli M. *The Fear of the Word: Censorship and Sex.* Metuchen, New Jersey: The Scarecrow Press, 1974.

Office for Intellectual Freedom. *Intellectual Freedom Manual.* Chicago: American Library Association, 1974.

Padover, Saul K., ed. *The Writings of Thomas Jefferson.* New York: Heritage Press, 1967.

Pastor, Ludwig. *The History of the Popes from the Close of the Middle Ages.* St. Louis: B. Hurder Company, 1898.

Plato. *The Republic, The Dialogues of Plato.* 2 volumes. Translated by B. Jowett. New York: Oxford University Press, 1892.

Postman, Neill and Weingartner, Charles. *Teaching as a Subversive Activity.* New York: Dell, 1969.

Rhode, Robert T. "Is Secular Humanism the Religion of the Public Schools?" In *Dealing with Censorship,* pp. 117-23. Edited by James E. Davis. Urbana, Illinois: National Council of Teachers of English, 1979.

Rugg, Harold. "A Study in Censorship: Good Concepts and Bad Words." In *The First Freedom: Liberty and Justice in the World of Books and Reading,* pp. 342-52. Edited by Robert B. Downs. Chicago: American Library Association, 1960.

Sagan, Carl. *Cosmos.* New York: Random House, 1980.

Schaffarzick, John. "Federal Curriculum Reform: A Crucible for Value Conflicts," pp. 3-24. In *Value Conflicts and Curriculum Issues: Lessons from Research and Experience.* Edited by John Schaffarzick and Gary Sykes. Berkley: McCutchan Publishing Corporation, 1979.

Schauer, Frederick F. *The Law of Obscenity.* Washington: Bureau of National Affairs, 1976.

Shakespeare, William. *The Complete Plays and Poems of Shakespeare.* Edited by William Allan Neilson and Charles Jarvis Hill. *The Tragedy of Richard the Sec-*

221

ond, pp. 598-631. Cambridge, Massachusetts: Houghton Mifflin Company, 1942.

Shugert, Diane P. "A Body of Well-Instructed Men and Women: Organizations Active for Intellectual Freedom." In *Dealing With Censorship,* pp. 187-201. Edited by James E. Davis. Urbana, Illinois: National Council of Teachers of English, 1979.

Sobel, Lester A., ed. *Pornography, Obscenity and the Law.* New York: Facts on File, 1979.

St. John-Stevas, Norman. *Obscenity and the Law.* London: Secker and Warberg, 1956.

Stanchfield, Jo M. "Trends—Not Destiny." In *Indoctrinate or Educate?* pp. 20-24. Edited by Thomas C. Hatcher and Lawrence G. Erickson. Newark, Delaware: International Reading Association, 1979.

Vonnegut, Kurt, Jr. *Slaughterhouse-Five.* New York: Delacorte Press, Inc., 1969.

Webster's New World Dictionary of the English Language, Second College Edition. New York: World Publishing Company, 1970.

Woods, Lemuel Byrd. *A Decade of Censorship in America: The Threat to Classrooms and Libraries, 1966-1975.* Metuchen, New Jersey: Scarecrow Press, 1979.

Wroth, Lawrence C. "Printing in the Colonial Period, 1638-1703." In *The Book in America,* pp. 44-48. Edited by Edward Lehmann Haupt. New York: Bowker, 1951.

Journals, Periodicals and Newspapers

"Academic Freedom in the Public Schools: The Right to Teach." *New York University Law Review* 48 (December 1973): 1176-1199.

American Library Association. "What to Do Before the Censor Comes—And After." *Newsletter on Intellectual Freedom* 21 (March 1972): 49-56.

Anderson, Wyatt W. "Evolutionist — Creationist Roundtable." *The Science Teacher* 43 (November 1976): 34-39.

Bogen, David S. "The Supreme Court's Interpretation of the Guarantee of Freedom of Speech." *Maryland Law Review* 35 (1976): 555-616.

Bradley, Julia Turnquist. "Censoring the School Library: Do Students Have the Right to Read?" *Connecticut Law Review* 10 (Spring 1978): 698-774.

Bradley, Julia Turnquist. "Constitutional Law — First Amendment — Right to Receive Information — Board of Education's Removal of Selected Books from Public School Library Violates Students' First Amendment Right to Receive Information." *Texas Law Review* 55 (Fall 1977): 511-523.

Bryson, Joseph E. "Academic Freedom and Due Process for Public School Teachers." *Educative Horizons,* Vol. 54, No. 1, Fall, 1975.

"Censorship on Rise Again in Schools." *U. S. News and World Report* 86 (June 4, 1979): 51.

Clark, Todd. "Editorial Reflections — Freedom to Teach and To Learn: Our Responsibility." *Social Education* 39 (April 1975): 202-04.

Clark, Todd. "The West Virginia Textbook Controversy: A Personal Account." *Social Education* 39 (April 1975): 216-19.

"Comment: School Boards, Schoolbooks and the Freedom to Learn." *Yale Law Review* 59 (1950): 953-54.

"Developments in the Law — Academic Freedom." *Harvard Law Review* 81 (1968): 1045-1158.

Eagles, William A. "Constitutional Law — Right of Public School Children to Receive Information — Minarcini v.

223

Strongsville City School District." *Wake Forest Law Review* 13 (1977): 834-41.

Geller, Evelyn. "The Librarian as Censor." *Library Journal* 101 (June 1970): 1255-58.

Gosse, Edmund. "The Censorship of Books." *English Review* 4 (March, 1910): 621-26.

Gyory, Richard. "The Constitutional Rights of Public School Pupils." *Fordham Law Review* 40 (1971): 201-37.

Hanser, Richard. "Shakespeare, Sex . . . And Dr. Bowdler." *The Saturday Review* 38 (April 23, 1955): 7-8.

Hirschoff, Mary-Michelle Upson. "Parents and the Public School Curriculum: Is There a Right to Have One's Child Excused from Objectionable Instruction?" *Southern California Law Review* 50 (1977): 871-957.

Hung, Pham Thein. "Parents Protest Textbooks." *Freedom of Information Center Report No. 401.* Columbia, Missouri: School of Journalism, University of Missouri (March 1979): 1-11.

Lyon, George W. "Book Burners in History." *The Saturday Review* 25 (August 15, 1942): 12-18.

Morrissett, Irving. "Curriculum Network Fourth Report: Controversies in the Classroom." *Social Education* 39 (April 1975): 246-52.

Moskowitz, Joel S. "Parental Rights and State Education." *Washington Law Review* 50 (1975): 623.

Nahmod, Sheldon H. "Controversy in the Classroom: The High School Teacher and Freedom of Expression." *George Washington Law Review* 39 (1971) 1030-45.

NEA Reporter. 19 (January/February 1980): 1.

Newsletter on Intellectual Freedom. 3 (January 25, 1955): 3; 6 (March 1957): 7; 6 (June 1957): 9; 7 (June 1958): 6; 10 (March 1961): 3; 11 (July 1962): 4-5; 20 (January 1971): 4; 20 (March 1971): 32-33, 60-61, 123, 130; 22 (May 1973): 52; 24 (July 1975): 103; 25 (November 1976): 145; 27 (November 1978): 138.

Nolte, M. Chester. "New Pig in the Parlor: Official Constraints on Indecent Words." *NOLPE School Law Journal* 9 (1980): 1-22.

O'Donnell, James J. "Censorship and the Publishers." *NASSP Bulletin* 59 (May 1975): 59-63.

O'Neil, Robert M. "Libraries, Liberties, and the First Amendment." *Cincinnati Law Review* 42 (1973): 209-51.

"Old Values Surface in Blume Country." *Bulletin of the Council on Interracial Books for Children* 7 (1977): 8-10.

Park, J. Charles. "The New Right: Threat to Democracy in Education." *Educational Leadership* 38 (November 1980): 146-49.

Parker, Barbara. "Your Schools May Be the Next Battlefield in the Crusade Against 'Improper' Textbooks." *American School Board Journal* 166 (June 1979): 27-30.

Procuniar, Pamela Ellen. "The Intellectual Rights of Children." *Wilson Library Bulletin* 51 (October 1976): 163-67.

"Progress, 1900-1915." *Social Hygiene* 11 (January 1916): 40-42.

"Removing Books from Schools: More Now than Anytime in the Last 25 Years." *American School Board Journal* 166 (June 1979): 22-24.

Rinsky, Lee and Schweikert. "In Defense of the 'New Realism' for Children and Adolescents." *Phi Delta Kappan* (February 1977): 472-75.

Schauer, Frederick S. "School Books, Lesson Plans, and the Constitution." *West Virginia Law Review* 78 (May 1976): 287-314.

Schember, Daniel M. "Textbook Censorship — The Validity

of School Board Rules." *Administrative Law Review* 28 (1976): 259-76.

"Some Isms Revisited; Answers from Blume Country: An Interview with Judy Blume." *Top of the News* 34 (Spring 1978): 233-43.

"Textbook Censors: You Can Survive Their Ire and Extinguish Their Fire." *The Executive Educator* 1 (July 1979): 25-27.

Woods, L. B. "Is Academic Freedom Dead in Public Schools?" *Phi Delta Kappan* 59 (October 1979): 104-06.

Legal Research Aids

American Jurisprudence. 2nd Vol. 68. Rochester, New York: Lawyers Cooperative Publishing Company, 1973.

Corpus Juris Secundum. Vols. 78 and 79. New York: The American Law Books Company, 1952.

National Reporter System. St. Paul, Minn.: West Publishing Company.
The Atlantic Reporter
The California Reporter
The Federal Reporter
The Federal Supplement
The New York Supplement
The Northeast Reporter
The Pacific Reporter
The Southeast Reporter
The Southern Reporter
The Supreme Court Report

Shepherd's Citations. Colorado Springs, Colorado: Shepherd's Citations, Inc., 1980.

Unpublished Materials

Bryson, Joseph E. *Current State-Church Issues.* Address delivered to the Virginia School Law Conference, Virginia Polytechnic Institute, Blacksburg, Virginia, November, 1980. (Typewritten.)

Christopher Ideas. The Christophers, 12 East 48th St., New York, New York, n.d. (Printed Sheet.)

Educational Research Analysts, Inc., Longview, Texas n.d. (Untitled Mimeographed Sheet.)

Educational Research Analysts, Inc., "Textbook Reviewing by Categories." Longview, Texas, n.d. (Mimeographed.)

Halley, Edward G. "Libraries and the Freedom of the Mind." Paper presented at the Cora Paul Bomar Lecture, University of North Carolina at Greensboro, 19 April 1980. (Mimeographed.)

McCoy, Ralph Edward. "Banned in Boston: The Development of Literary Censorship." Ph.D. Dissertation, University of Illinois, 1956.

Unpublished survey of the Intellectual Freedom Committee of the North Carolina Library Association, April 1979. Conducted by Phil Morris and Martha E. Davis. (Typewritten.)

TABLE OF CASES

Section references to principal cases are in italics.

A

Abrams v. United States, 250 U.S. 616, 40 S. Ct. 17, 63 L. Ed. 1173 (1919) — § 3.1B, n. 42.

Adler v. Board of Educ., 342 U.S. 485, 72 S. Ct. 380, 96 L. Ed. 517 (1952) — § 4.1, n. 6.

Albaum v. Carey, 283 F. Supp. 3 (E.D.N.Y. 1968) — § 3.1A, nn. 23, 24.

B

Besig v. United States, 208 F.2d 142 (9th Cir. 1953) — § 3.2, nn. 127, 128.

Bicknell v. Vergennes Union High School Bd. of Directors, 475 F. Supp. 615 (D. Vt. 1979), aff'd, 638 F.2d 438 (2d Cir. 1980) — § 3.3A, nn. 220, 223, 225; *§ 4.3*.

Board of Educ. v. Pico, Case No. 80-2043, 50 L.W. 4831 (1982) — § 3.1B, n. 52; § 3.1C, n. 62; § 3.3B, nn. 308-316, 318-320; *§ 4.2*.

Book Named "John Cleland's Memoirs of a Woman of Pleasure" v. Attorney General, 383 U.S. 413, 86 S. Ct. 975, 16 L. Ed. 2d 1 (1966) — § 3.2, nn. 144, 152.

Brown v. Board of Educ., 347 U.S. 483, 74 S. Ct. 686, 98 L. Ed. 873 (1954) — § 3.1A, nn. 16, 17; § 3.1B, n. 32; § 3.1D, n. 80.

Brubaker v. Board of Educ., 502 F.2d 973 (7th Cir. 1974) — § 3.3A, nn. 202-204, 206, 208, 209, 227.

Butler v. Michigan, 352 U.S. 380, 77 S. Ct. 524, 1 L. Ed. 2d 412 (1957) — § 3.2, nn. 129, 130.

C

Cary v. Board of Educ., 427 F. Supp. 945 (D. Colo. 1977), aff'd, 598 F.2d 535 (10th Cir. 1979) — § 3.3A, nn. 211-214; *§ 4.3*.

Cary v. Board of Educ., Slip Opinion Nos. 77-1297, 77-1298 (10th Cir. 1979) — § 3.3A, nn. 210, 215-219.

Celestine v. Lafayette Parish School Bd., 284 So. 2d 650 (La. 1973) — § 3.3B, n. 263.

Commonwealth v. Gordon, 66 Pa. Dist. & Co. 101 (1949) — § 2.4, n. 85.

Commonwealth v. Feigenbaum, 166 Pa. Super. 120, 70 A.2d 389 (1950) — § 3.2, n. 125.
Commonwealth v. Holmes, 17 Mass (1921) — § 2.4, nn. 80, 81.
Commonwealth v. Isenstadt, 318 Mass. 543, 62 N.E.2d 840 (1945) — § 3.2, nn. 121, 122, 134.
Commonwealth v. Sharpless, 2 S. & R. 91 (Pa. Supp. Ct. 1815) — § 2.4, n. 77.

D

Daniel v. Waters, 399 F. Supp. 510 (M.D. Tenn. 1975) — § 2.4, n. 10.
Doubleday & Co. v. New York, 335 U.S. 848 (1948) — § 3.2, n. 124.

E

Epperson v. Arkansas, 393 U.S. 97, 89 S. Ct. 266, 21 L. Ed. 2d 228 (1968) — § 3.0, nn. 3, 5; § 3.1E, nn. 94, 96, 97; § 3.3A, n. 170; § 4.4, n. 128; *§ 4.4.*

F

Federal Communications Comm'n v. Pacifica Found., 438 U.S. 726, 98 S. Ct. 3026, 57 L. Ed. 2d 1073 (1978) — § 3.1B, nn. 49, 51.

G

Ginsberg v. New York, 390 U.S. 629, 88 S. Ct. 1274, 20 L. Ed. 2d 195 (1968) — § 3.2, nn. 145, 146, 149; § 3.3A, n. 174; § 3.3B, n. 245; § 4.2, n. 25.
Glaser v. Marietta, 351 F. Supp. 555 (W.D. Pa. 1972) — § 3.1B, nn. 86, 87.
Goss v. Lopez, 419 U.S. 565, 95 S. Ct. 729, 42 L. Ed. 2d 725 (1975) — § 3.1B, n. 36.

H

Hannegan v. Esquire, Inc., 327 U.S. 146, 66 S. Ct. 456, 90 L. Ed. 586 (1946) — § 3.1C, n. 59.
Harris v. Mechanicville Cent. School Dist., 45 N.Y.2d 279, 408 N.Y.S.2d 384, 380 N.E.2d 213 (1978) — § 3.3B, nn. 263, 264.
Harris v. Mechanicville Cent. School Dist., 86 Misc. 2d 144, 382 N.Y.S.2d 251 (1976), *rev'd,* 57 A.D.2d 231, 394 N.Y.S.2d 302 (1977) — § 3.3B, nn. 260-262.

I

In re Gault, 387 U.S. 1, 87 S. Ct. 1428, 18 L. Ed. 2d 527 (1967) —
§ 3.1B, nn. 32, 35.

J

Jacobellis v. Ohio, 378 U.S. 184, 84 S. Ct. 1676, 12 L. Ed. 2d 793
(1964) — § 3.2, nn. 141-143.

K

Kaplan v. California, 413 U.S. 115, 93 S. Ct. 2680, 37 L. Ed. 2d 492
(1973) — § 3.2, n. 144.
Keefe v. Geanakos, 305 F. Supp. 1091 (D. Mass.), *rev'd and
remanded,* 418 F.2d 359 (1st Cir. 1969) — § 3.1C, n. 63;
§ 3.3A, nn. 192, 195, 198; § 3.3B, nn. 233-240; *§ 4.1.*
Kent v. United States, 383 U.S. 541, 86 S. Ct. 1045, 16 L. Ed. 2d 84
(1966) — § 3.1B, n. 32.
Keyishian v. Board of Regents, 385 U.S. 589, 87 S. Ct. 675, 17 L.
Ed. 2d 629 (1967) — § 3.1A, nn. 18, 20, 21, 28; *§ 4.1.*
Kleindienst v. Mandel, 408 U.S. 753, 92 S. Ct. 2576, 33 L. Ed. 2d
683 (1972) — § 3.1B, nn. 45, 47.
Kovacs v. Cooper, 336 U.S. 77, 69 S. Ct. 448, 93 L. Ed 513 (1949) —
§ 3.1C, n. 57.

L

Lamont v. Postmaster General, 381 U.S. 301 (1965) — § 3.1B, n.
52.
Lemon v. Kurtzman, 403 U.S. 602, 91 S. Ct. 2105, 29 L. Ed. 2d 745
(1971) — § 3.1E, n. 114.
Lindros v. Governing Bd., 108 Cal. Rptr. 185, 9 Cal. 3d 524, 510
P.2d 361 (1972), *cert. denied,* 414 U.S. 1112 (1973) — § 3.0, n.
3; § 3.1A, n. 28; § 3.3A, nn. 191, 196, 199-201.

M

Mailloux v. Kiley, 323 F. Supp. 1387 (D. Mass.), *aff'd,* 448 F.2d
1242 (1st Cir. 1971) — § 3.0, n. 3; § 3.1A, n. 28; § 3.1C,
n. 67; § 3.3A, nn. 197, 207.
Martin v. City of Struthers, 319 U.S. 141, 63 S. Ct. 862, 87 L.Ed
1313 (1943) — § 3.1B, n. 52.
McColum v. Board of Educ., 333 U.S. 203, 68 S. Ct. 461, 92 L. Ed.
649 (1948) — § 3.1E, nn. 92, 93.

McLean v. Arkansas Bd. of Educ., 529 F. Supp. 1255 (E.D. Ark. 1982) — § 2.4, n. 100; § 3.1E, n. 97; § 4.4, n. 134.

Medeiros v. Kiyosaki, 52 Hawaii 436, 478 P.2d 314 (1970) — § 3.1E, nn. 111-113; § 3.3A, nn. 163, 164, 167; § 4.4., n. 130; *§ 4.4.*

Meitzer v. Board of Pub. Instruction of Orange City, 548 F.2d 559 (5th Cir. 1977) — § 3.1E, n. 102.

Meyer v. Nebraska, 262 U.S. 390, 43 S. Ct. 625, 67 L. Ed. 1042 (1923) — § 3.1A, nn. 9, 10, 28; § 3.1D, n. 75; § 3.3A, n. 165; *§ 4.1;* § 4.3, nn. 102-104; § 4.4, nn. 125, 127.

Miller v. California, 413 U.S. 15, 93 S. Ct. 2607, 37 L. Ed. 2d 419 (1973) — § 1.1, nn. 24-26; § 3.1B, n. 44; § 3.1C, n. 60; § 3.2, nn. 144, 150-151, 153-155; § 3.3B, n. 316.

Minarcini v. Strongsville City School Dist., 384 F. Supp. 698 (N.D. Ohio 1974), *aff'd in part, rev'd in part,* 541 F.2d 577 (6th Cir. 1976) — § 3.1C, n. 68; § 3.3B, nn. 251, 252, 254-256, 259, 278, 301, 305; § 4.2, n. 28; *§ 4.2.*

Moore v. Gaston County Bd. of Educ., 357 F. Supp. 1037 (W.D.N.C. 1973) — § 3.1A, n. 28.

Murray v. Curlett, 228 Md. 239, 179 A.2d 698 (1962) — § 3.1E, n. 101.

P

Parducci v. Rutland, 316 F. Supp. 352 (M.D. Ala. 1970) — § 3.1A, n. 28; § 3.3A, nn. 193, 194; § 3.3B, nn. 241-243, 247; *§ 4.1.*

Paris Adult Theatre I v. Slaton, 413 U.S. 49, 93 S. Ct. 2628, 37 L. Ed. 2d 446 (1973) — § 3.2, nn. 144, 150; § 3.3A, n. 205.

Parker v. Board of Educ., 237 F. Supp. 222 (D. Md.), *aff'd,* 348 F.2d 464 (4th Cir. 1965), *cert. denied,* 382 U.S. 1030 (1966) — § 3.3A, nn. 159-162.

Pico v. Board of Educ., 474 F. Supp. 387 (E.D.N.Y. 1979), *rev'd and remanded,* 638 F.2d 404 (2d Cir. 1980) — § 3.1C, n. 62; § 3.3B, nn. 294-300, 307; *§ 4.2.*

Pierce v. Society of Sisters of the Holy Names of Jesus and Mary, 268 U.S. 510, 45 S. Ct. 671, 69 L. Ed. 1070 (1925) — § 3.1D, nn. 77, 78; § 3.3A, n. 166.

Pratt v. Independent School Dist. No. 831, 670 F.2d 771 (8th Cir. 1982) — § 3.1B, n. 52; § 3.3B, nn. 284-293; *§ 4.2.*

Presidents Council, Dist. 25 v. Community School Bd. No. 25, 457 F.2d 289 (2d Cir.), *cert. denied,* 409 U.S. 998 (1972) — § 3.0, n. 3; § 3.3A, nn. 168, 172, 173, 175, 176, 178-181, 221, 222; § 3.3B, nn. 253, 267, 304; § 4.2, n. 35; *§ 4.3.*

R

Red Lion Broadcasting Co. v. Federal Communications Comm'n, 395 U.S. 367, 89 S. Ct. 1794, 23 L. Ed. 2d 371 (1969) — § 3.3B, n. 271.

Regina v. Hicklin, 3 L.R.-Q.B. 360 (1869) — § 2.4, nn. 92, 95; § 3.2, nn. 115, 116, 119, 139.

Right to Read Defense Comm. v. School Comm., 454 F. Supp. 703 (D. Mass. 1978) — § 3.3B, nn. 265, 266, 268, 269, 302; *§ 4.2;* § 4.3, n. 109.

Rosenberg v. Board of Educ., 196 Misc. 542, 92 N.Y.S.2d 344 (Sup. Ct. 1949) — § 3.1C, n. 61; § 3.1E, n. 108.

Roth v. United States, 354 U.S. 476, 77 S. Ct. 1304, 1 L. Ed. 2d 1498 (1957) — § 3.1C, n. 60; § 3.2, nn. 131, 132, 135-138, 140, 147, 148, 156-158; § 3.3B, n. 244.

S

Salvail v. Nashua Bd. of Educ., 469 F. Supp. 1269 (D.N.H. 1979) — § 3.3B, nn. 272-277, 280, 303; § 4.2, n. 29; § 4.3, n. 110.

Schneider v. State, 308 U.S. 147, 60 S. Ct. 146, 84 L. Ed. 155 (1939) — § 3.1C, n. 69.

School Dist. of Abington Township v. Schempp, 374 U.S. 203 (1963) — § 3.1E, nn. 98-100; § 3.3A, n. 186; § 4.4, n. 135.

Scopes v. State, 154 Tenn. 105, 289 S.W. 363 (1927) — § 3.1E, n. 95.

Sheck v. Baileyville School Comm., 530 F. Supp. 679 (D. Me. 1982) — § 3.3B, nn. 281-283.

Spence v. Washington, 418 U.S. 405, 94 S. Ct. 2727, 41 L. Ed. 2d 842 (1974) — § 3.1C, n. 70.

Sterzing v. Fort Bend Indep. School Dist., 376 F. Supp. 657 (S.D. Tex. 1972), *vacated and remanded,* 496 F.2d 92 (5th Cir. 1974) — § 3.3B, nn. 248-250.

Sweezy v. New Hampshire, 354 U.S. 234, 77 S. Ct. 1203, 1 L. Ed. 2d 1311 (1957) — § 3.1A, nn. 13, 14, 28.

T

Tinker v. Des Moines Indep. Community School Dist., 393 U.S. 503, 89 S. Ct. 733, 21 L. Ed. 2d 731 (1969) — § 1.1, nn. 19, 20, 22, 23; § 3.1A, nn. 26-28; § 3.1B, nn. 32, 33, 38, 39, 41, 53; § 3.1C, n. 64; § 3.1D, n. 82; § 3.3A, n. 177; § 3.3B, nn. 246, 257, 270; *§ 4.1;* § 4.1, n. 19; § 4.2, nn. 20, 26.

Todd v. Rochester Community Schools, 41 Mich. App. 320, 200 N.W.2d 90 (1972) — § 3.1E, n. 109; § 3.3A, nn. 182, 184, 185, 187-190; § 4.4, n. 129; *§ 4.4.*

Torcaso v. Watkins, 367 U.S. 488, 81 S. Ct. 1680, 6 L. Ed. 2d 982 (1961) — § 2.4, nn. 212-214.

U

United States v. Associated Press, 326 U.S. 1, 65 S. Ct. 1416, 89 L. Ed. 1954 (1945) — § 3.1A, n. 19.

United States v. Bennett, 16 Blatch 338, Fed. Case 14, 571 (1879) — § 3.0, n. 1; § 3.18, n. 43.

United States v. Kennerley, 209 F. 119 (S.D.N.Y. 1913) — § 3.2, nn. 117, 118, 133.

United States v. One Book Called "Ulysses," 5 F. Supp. 182 (S.D.N.Y. 1933), *aff'd,* 72 F.2d 705 (2d Cir. 1934) — § 3.2, n. 120.

United States v. 12 200-Ft. Reels of Super 8 mm. Film, 413 U.S. 123, 93 S. Ct. 2665, 37 L. Ed. 2d 500 (1973) — § 3.2, nn. 144, 150.

United States v. Orito, 413 U.S. 139, 93 S. Ct. 2674, 37 L. Ed. 2d 513 (1973) — § 3.2, nn. 144, 150.

United States v. Seeger, 380 U.S. 163, 85 S. Ct. 850, 13 L. Ed. 2d 733 (1965) — § 2.4, n. 215.

V

Valent v. New Jersey State Bd. of Educ., 114 N.J. Super. 63, 274 A.2d 832 (1971) — § 3.1E, n. 107.

Virginia State Bd. of Pharmacy v. Virginia Citizens Consumer Council, Inc., 425 U.S. 748, 96 S. Ct. 1817, 48 L. Ed. 2d 346 (1976) — § 3.1B, nn. 46, 48; § 3.3B, nn. 258, 279, 306; *§ 4.2.*

W

Walz v. Tax Comm'n, 397 U.S. 664, 90 S. Ct. 1409, 25 L. Ed. 2d 697 (1970) — § 3.1E, n. 114.

West Virginia State Bd. of Educ. v. Barnette, 319 U.S. 624, 63 S. Ct. 1178, 87 L. Ed. 1628 (1943) — § 3.1C, n. 58; § 3.1E, n. 104.

Williams v. Board of Educ., 388 F. Supp. 93 (S.D.W.V. 1975) — § 3.1E, n. 110.

Winters v. New York, 333 U.S. 507, 68 S. Ct. 665, 92 L. Ed. 840 (1948) — § 3.2, n. 123.

Wisconsin v. Yoder, 406 U.S. 205, 92 S. Ct. 1526, 32 L. Ed. 2d 15 (1972) — § 3.1B, nn. 83, 85; § 3.1E, n. 105; § 4.4, n. 126; § 4.4.

Wood v. Strickland, 420 U.S. 308, 95 S. Ct. 992, 43 L. Ed. 2d 214 (1974) — § 3.1B, n. 37; § 3.1D, n. 85.

Z

Zykan v. Warsaw Community School Corp., 631 F.2d 1300 (7th Cir. 1980) — § 3.3A, nn. 226, 228-232.

Index

A

ACADEMIC FREEDOM.
Definitions, §1.4.
Public school teachers, §3.1.
Review of court decisions, §4.1.
Review of court decisions,
Public school teachers. §4.1.

C

CASES.
Constitutional rights.
Cases supporting constitutional rights, §3.3.
Cases supporting school board action, §3.3.
Religious freedom of public school students, §3.1.
Parents.
Review of court decisions, §4.4.
Review of court decisions.
Academic freedom of public school teachers, §4.1.
Introduction, §4.0.
Parental rights to direct the education of children, §4.4.
School boards.
Right to select and remove library and instructional materials, §4.3.
Students' rights to read, inquire, and receive information, §4.2.
School boards.
Review of court decisions, §4.3.
Students.
Review of court decisions, §4.2.
Teachers.
Review of court decisions.
Academic freedom of public school teachers, §4.1.

COLONIAL AMERICA.
Historical perspective, §2.2.

CONCLUDING STATEMENT, §5.3.

CONCLUSIONS, §5.1.

CONSTITUTIONAL RIGHTS.
Cases supporting constitutional rights, §3.3.

CONSTITUTIONAL RIGHTS—Cont'd
Religious freedom of public school students, §3.1.

D

DEFINITIONS.
Academic freedom, §1.4.
Censor, §1.4.
Censorship, §1.4.
Evolution of legal definition of obscenity, §3.2.
Obscenity, §1.4.
Evolution of legal definition of obscenity, §3.2.
Selection, §1.4.
Terms, §1.4.

H

HISTORICAL PERSPECTIVE.
American colonies, §2.2.
Colonial America, §2.2.
Eighteenth-Century America, §2.3.
Generally, §2.1.
Introduction, §2.0.
Nineteenth Century America, §2.4.
Summary, §2.5.
Twentieth Century America, §2.4.

I

INTRODUCTION, §3.0.
Coverage of issues involved, §1.3.
Definition of terms, §1.4.
Organization of issues involved, §1.3.
Overview, §1.0.
Questions to be answered, §1.2.
Review of court decisions, §4.0.
Review of the literature, §2.0.
Status of censorship practices in the public schools, §1.1.

O

OBSCENITY.
Definitions, §1.4.
Evolution of legal definition of obscenity, §3.2.
Evolution of legal definition, §3.2.

OBSCENITY—Cont'd
Historical perspective on censorship, §2.1.
OVERVIEW, §1.0.

P

PARENTS.
  Cases.
    Review of court decisions, §4.4.
    Right to direct education of children, §3.1.
    Status of censorship practices in the public schools, §1.1.
POLICIES.
  Recommended school board policies, §5.4.
PUBLIC SCHOOLS.
  Library and instructional materials.
    Censorship cases, §3.3.
      Cases supporting constitutional rights, §3.3.
      Cases supporting school board action, §3.3.
    Definitions.
      Evolution of legal definition of obscenity, §3.2.
    Framework for analyzing.
      Academic freedom of public school teachers, §3.1.
      Parental rights to direct education of children, §3.1.
      Religious freedom of public school students, §3.1.
      Right of students to read and receive information, §3.1.
      School board authority to select and remove materials, §3.1.
    Introduction, §3.0.
    Obscenity.
      Evolution of legal definition, §3.2.
    Parents.
      Right to direct education of children, §3.1.
    Religious freedom.
      Students in public schools, §3.1.
    Right of students to read and receive information, §3.1.
    School boards.
      Authority to select and remove library and instructional
        materials, §3.1.
    Students.
      Religious freedom, §3.1.
    Summary, §3.4.
    Teachers.
      Academic freedom of teachers, §3.1.
  School boards.
    See SCHOOL BOARDS.

R

RECOMMENDATIONS, §5.2.
RELIGIOUS FREEDOM.
Public school students, §3.1.

S

SCHOOL BOARDS.
Authority to select and remove library and instructional materials, §3.1.
Cases.
Review of court decisions, §4.3.
Recommended policy for selection of library and instructional materials, §5.4.
Status of censorship practices in the public schools, §1.1.

STUDENTS.
Cases.
Review of court decisions, §4.2.
Religious freedom, §3.1.
Right of students to read and receive information, §3.1.
Religious freedom, §3.1.
Status of censorship practices in the public schools, §1.1.

SUMMARY.
Concluding statement, §5.3.
Conclusions, §5.1.
Generally, §5.0.
Recommendations, §5.2.
Recommended school board policy, §5.4.
Review of the literature, §2.5.

T

TEACHERS.
Academic freedom of public school teachers, §3.1.
Review of court decisions, §4.1.
Cases.
Review of court decisions.
Academic freedom of public school teachers, §4.1.
Status of censorship practices in the public schools, §1.1.

TERMS.
Definitions, §1.4.